Algeria

Algeria

BY MARTIN HINTZ

Enchantment of the World
Second Series

Children's Press®

A Division of Scholastic Inc.

NEW YORK   TORONTO   LONDON   AUCKLAND   SYDNEY
MEXICO CITY   NEW DELHI   HONG KONG
DANBURY, CONNECTICUT

Dedication

To Algeria's Young People

Frontispiece: Tuareg travels with his camels near the oasis town of Djanet.

Consultant: Phillip C. Naylor, Department of History, Marquette University, Milwaukee, Wisconsin

Please note: All statistics are as up-to-date as possible at the time of publication.

Book production by Herman Adler Design

Library of Congress Cataloging-in-Publication Data

Hintz, Martin.
  Algeria / by Martin Hintz.
    p. cm. — (Enchantment of the world. Second series)
  Includes bibliographical references and index.
  ISBN 0-516-24855-3
  1. Algeria—Juvenile literature. I. Title. II. Series.
  DT275.H56 2005
  965—dc22   2005007825

Acknowledgments

The author wishes to thank legal expert and journalist Dahmène Touchent; author William Langewiesche who knows so much about camels, rock paintings, and sand; Sahara observer Ralph A. Bagnold; and adventurers such as Henrik de Leeuw, Scott Wayne, Peter Fuchs, Edith Fischer, and Andreas Kronenberg whose love of Algeria is evident in their journals.

The author also appreciates the work done by the intrepid travelers at Lonely Planet Books and editor Doré Ogrizek, who shepherded a marvelous stable of artists and writers for *World in Color: North Africa*. Another thank you goes to Kamel Kharchi of the Algerian embassy in Washington, D.C.

Thanks also to Professor Mark Tessler, director of the International Institute at the University of Michigan–Ann Arbor, and to Marilyn Jenkins, resource technician at the International Trade Center of the Waukesha County Technical College. The author also extends thanks to University of Wisconsin–Milwaukee interns Sherrie Baker and Kat O'Connell and the staff of the Milwaukee Central Library.

A special nod goes to Professor Abdallah Bedaida, vice rector of the University of Algiers and a member of Social and Economic National Council of Algeria. His insights, observations, and commentary while reviewing this manuscript were extremely helpful.

Cover photo:
Camels in
the desert

Contents

Kerzaz Oasis

Algerian girls

Flying Over a Vibrant World

8

THE AIR ALGÉRIE PLANE TAKES OFF FROM PARIS, FRANCE. It flies south, eventually crossing the choppy green waters of the Mediterranean Sea before circling above Algiers, the capital of Algeria. Passengers in the plane can spot EgyptAir and Royal Air Maroc flights in the distance. The three planes swoop down like hawks toward Houari Boumediene International Airport lying just ahead.

From this aerial vantage point, passengers can see how Algiers carpets a rocky hillside. The city is a jumbled mix of old and new. The narrow alleys of the casbah, the neighborhood of the old fortress, crawl along like zigzagging snakes. Downtown, modern buildings and wide plazas crowd around the harbor.

If the plane continued to fly over Algeria instead of landing at the airport, passengers would see a marvelously rich landscape, with towering palm trees and acres of farmland beyond the sprawl of the capital. Even from high in the air, it seems almost possible to smell the thick

Opposite: **A villager in traditional dress makes her way through the Algerian countryside.**

Algiers as seen from Hydra Hill

sweetness of oleander and other flowers emanating from secret gardens. Villages dot the countryside below, with mud-walled buildings blending into the ground. Passengers also would see a high, barren plateau followed by the sharp peaks and valleys of craggy mountains.

Then comes the Sahara Desert, which covers 3.5 million square miles (9 million square kilometers) and is still growing. The desert landscape is constantly moving and changing. Sand urged along by strong, hot wind fills the air. Anyone crossing the desert needs a scarf as face protection because the blowing sand makes it difficult to breathe. Viewed from above, the desert appears to hold no life. But Algerians live there, making their way from oasis to oasis by camel and four-wheel-drive vehicles.

Camel caravans are still sometimes used in the Sahara Desert near Djanet.

It is easy to get lost in the sandy desert because of the constantly shifting sand. From the air, especially at night, the sand looks almost like an ocean. Traveling during the cool darkness, nomads used to find their way by following the stars. Today, modern travelers can use global positioning instruments to pinpoint where they are.

Children in the oasis village of Taghit don't need such sophisticated equipment to find a good time. They just walk out their back doors. Their town is surrounded by some of the most spectacular sand dunes in Algeria. The children take pieces of tin, cardboard, or plastic to the top of the sandy peaks and slide down on them. This sport is as much fun as sledding down snowy hills.

The plane flies on, passing over oil and natural-gas fields with their pumping machinery and flaming towers burning off excess gases. Here and there are more dots of greenery—signs of water wells that bring life to people and animals living in remote corners of the country.

Algerians have come to terms with the unforgiving desert. People live in domed houses, in which the heat rises, so the interior doesn't seem as warm. Farmers in the Souf region grow crops in one of the hottest parts of the Sahara. Daytime

Sunrise in the Ahaggar Mountains of the Sahara Desert

temperatures regularly reach 120° Fahrenheit (50° Celsius) here. It can be so hot that touching a door handle can burn the skin. Men dig holes in the sand with shovels, using palm leaves to keep the sand from sliding back. Date palms and other plants are planted in these holes. Their roots reach deep down under the surface to find hidden water. Sometimes, the pits are so deep that only the tops of the trees appear above the dunes.

The plane flies on, looking for the small airfield at Tamanrasset, nearly 1,000 miles (1,600 km) south of Algiers. The city of almost forty thousand is a servicing point for trucks and camel caravans traveling in the desert. Along Avenue Emir Abd al-Qadir, the city's main street, modern vehicles mingle with lanky brown camels carrying nomadic Tuareg people. Off to the east, the Ahaggar Mountains can just be seen on the horizon. From Tamanrasset, passengers can transfer to another plane and fly 259 miles (416 km) south to the Algerian border post at In-Guezzam. They may have to wait, however. There is only one flight a week to In-Guezzam, the last village in Algeria before crossing into Niger, the country to the south.

Whether they live in the urban north or the remote south, Algerians are fiercely proud of their land. Though Algeria

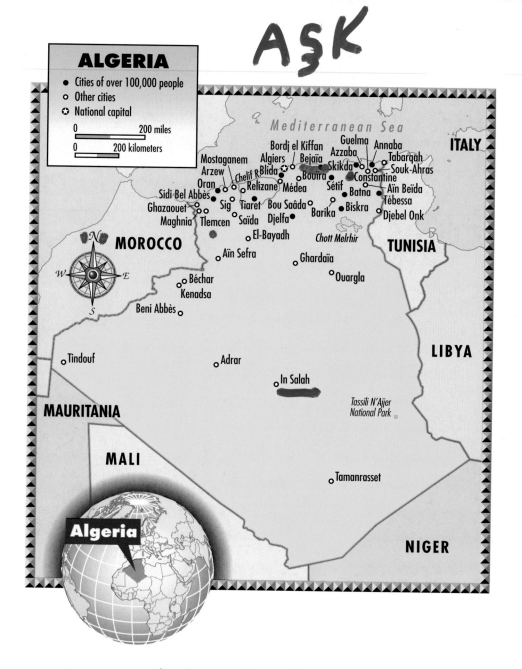

ALGERIA

- • Cities of over 100,000 people
- ○ Other cities
- ✪ National capital

0 ——— 200 miles
0 ——— 200 kilometers

Mediterranean Sea

ITALY

Bordj el Kiffan Guelma Annaba
Mostaganem Algiers Bejaïa Azzaba Tabarqah
Arzew Blida Skikda Souk-Ahras
Chelif R. Relizane Bouira Constantine
Oran Médea Sétif Aïn Beïda
Sidi-Bel Abbès Batna Tébessa
Ghazaouet Sig Tiaret Bou Saâda Biskra Djebel Onk
Maghnia Tlemcen Saïda Djelfa Barika

Chott Melrhir TUNISIA

El-Bayadh

Aïn Sefra Ghardaïa

Ouargla

MOROCCO

Béchar
Kenadsa

Beni Abbès

LIBYA

Tindouf Adrar

In Salah

Tassili N'Ajjer National Park

MAURITANIA

MALI

Tamanrasset

NIGER

Algeria

sometimes appears harsh, it is also explosively beautiful, with
sunrises and sunsets that make the sky drip with vibrant colors.
It is a nation rich in history, natural resources, and landscapes.
But it is the citizens of Algeria who are the real treasure.

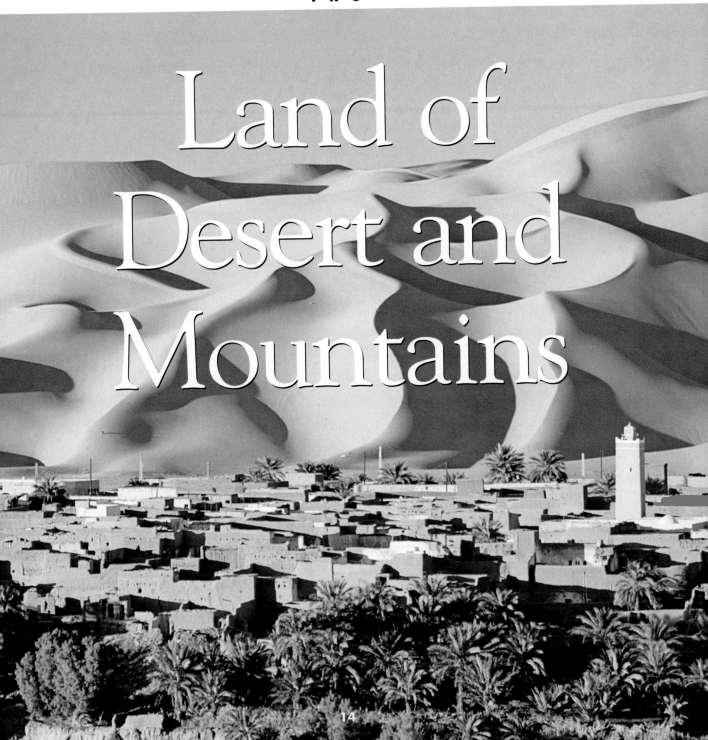

Land of Desert and Mountains

LGERIA LIES ALONG THE ROCK-RIBBED COAST OF North Africa. It is a beautifully rugged country, a marvelous mix of mountains tickling the sky and massive sand dunes flowing over a wide expanse of desert. Algeria is the second-largest country in Africa and the eleventh-largest country in the world, sprawling over 919,595 square miles (2,381,741 sq km). It is equal in size to western Europe and about one-quarter the size of the United States.

Opposite: **Oasis town of Kerzaz**

The Sahara Desert's Gourara Valley

Underground Wonders

The Grotte Karstique de Ghar Boumâaza, the largest known cave network in Africa, was discovered in 1931 near Tlemcen. It follows the Tafna River under the Tlemcen Mountains. Only about 10 miles (15.5 km) of the deep, dark passageways have been explored.

Three species of bats have been discovered inside the caverns. The permanent presence of water has allowed villages to be established above the caves. The locals tap into the water reservoir to irrigate their fields in this arid region.

The Mediterranean Sea is Algeria's northern border. To the east are the countries of Libya and Tunisia. On the west sit Mauritania, Morocco, and Western Sahara. To the south are Niger and Mali.

The Coast

Algeria has no lakes or rivers of importance, but it does have 750 miles (1,200 km) of coastline washed by the gray-green waters of the Mediterranean Sea. A strong current rushes eastward along the North African shore before crashing against Algeria's rocky coast, which has few good harbors. During the summer, an east wind carries thick fog, while winter storms from the north blow straight against the coast. Historically,

Algeria's coast is beautiful, but difficult to navigate.

these conditions made the Algerian coast a dangerous place to sail.

Algeria's High Plateaus are dry and rough.

Lowlands and Mountains

Most of Algeria is dry and windy. Crops can be grown on only about 3 percent of the land. Around 13 percent of Algeria is pastureland, and about 2 percent is forested. Most of the rest of the land is desert.

Algeria is divided into three major sections. The first region is the Tell, from the Arabic word meaning "hill." This fertile lowland strip extends along nearly the entire Mediterranean coast. This is where most Algerians live. The second region is the High Plateaus. From the air, the plateaus look like someone tossed rumpled blankets on a bed between the Tell and the Saharan Atlas Mountains. The plateaus average between 1,300 and 4,300 feet (400 and 1,300 meters) above sea level. They

Eroded mountains rise above the valley of the Oued Ouezzene

are actually the remains of ancient mountains that eroded over tens of thousands of years from the wind and rain.

The Saharan Atlas Range marks the dividing line between the High Plateaus and the Sahara Desert. The range is formed out of three massifs, or high ridges, called the Ksour, the Amour, and the Oulad Nail. These mountains are prone to severe earthquakes and dangerous mudslides. Nevertheless, the herdsmen who live in the region eagerly anticipate rain because it creates healthy pastureland for their flocks of hungry goats and sheep. Streams flow down the slopes of these massifs and disappear into the Sahara. The water then bubbles underground to supply wells on the northern edge of the desert. Among the most prominent oases irrigated by these underground waterways is the date-growing town of Biskra. Another is Laghouat, noted for its rug and tapestry industry. A third is dusty Béchar, a provincial capital and a mining center.

The Sahara

The wind-swept, sun-baked Sahara is the third major geographical region of Algeria. This formidable desert covers about 80 percent of Algeria but is home to only 3 percent of the nation's people. Temperatures in the Sahara often reach 120°F (49°C) during the day and plunge to almost freezing at night. Most Saharan sand dunes are 7 to 16 feet (2 to 5 m) high, but in some places they are taller than the palm trees. The dunes sweep in brown waves across the northern quarter of this desolate but beautiful region. Not all the Sahara is sand, however. Rocks and boulders litter the ground like giant marbles in some areas. The country's highest point, Mount Tahat, rears its rock-crowned head 9,573 feet (2,918 m) in the Ahaggar Mountains of southeastern Algeria.

The Sahara Desert in the Ahaggar region contains dramatic sandstone rock formations.

During Algeria's spring and summer, a hot, dry wind called the sirocco blows north from the interior of the Sahara. The wind, which picks up gritty sand from the desert, coats everything with a thin film of choking dust. The sirocco even crosses the wide Mediterranean Sea to the European coast, picking up moisture as it travels over water and causing fog and "red rain." These rainstorms leave behind red dust. If not quickly cleaned away, this dust can damage sensitive equipment such as computers and engine parts. When the dusty sirocco is blowing, it is sometimes impossible to see more than 100 feet (30 m) ahead.

The Shapes of Dunes

Algeria is home to several different kinds of sand dunes. The *barchan* (right) is found throughout the Great Eastern Erg, a vast sandy region that covers about one-quarter of Algeria. The barchan is a crescent-shaped sand pile caused by wind blowing in one direction. This dune has a sloping back and a steep leeward side—the direction toward which the wind blows. Sand grains tumble down the front of the dune, and these continual small avalanches cause the barchan to advance. The barchan dunes link to form horizon-to-horizon stretches of rolling, tumbling sand.

In other areas of the desert, where the wind changes direction, the dunes form long, curving patterns that Algerians call *seif*. This is an Arabic word for "sword." These dunes remind some people of the long, curved blades once used in the region.

A third, star-shaped pattern is formed when the wind blows from all points on the compass. In these places, the sand does not move as much, but it does pile upward into shapes like starfish. Each arm of the dune can reach out for miles in any one direction.

Looking at Algeria's Cities

Oran (below), Algeria's second-largest city, has about 1,100,000 residents. The city sits on a gracefully arching bay along the Mediterranean Sea in western Algeria. It was founded in the tenth century by Arab sailors from Spain. The Spanish eventually invaded Algeria and occupied the city in 1509, but they abandoned the city in 1791, after a massive earthquake. The city was next occupied by the Ottomans, who remained until the French arrived in 1831. After Algeria became independent, more than two hundred thousand Europeans fled Oran.

Today, Oran is one of Algeria's major port cities, with ferry service to France and Spain. Oran enjoys mild temperatures. The average temperature is 71°F (22°C) in June and 51°F (11°C) in January. The city's

Demaeght Museum has many rare animal fossils from prehistoric Algeria. The Promenade Ibn Badis has a garden and walkway built in 1847. Many trees have been planted along the way, making it a favorite place for a shady stroll in the day's heat.

Constantine (above), Algeria's third-largest city, is home to about 808,000 people. The city was built in A.D. 313 by the Roman emperor Constantine the Great on the same site where the ancient Numidian city of Cirta once stood. Constantine is built on a spit of land sticking far out into the sea. Sharp cliffs fall away on two sides. Constantine is a center for the manufacture of leather, woolen, and linen products. The Palace of Ahmed Bey, which was built in 1835, is one of the major architectural wonders of the city. The Place de Martyrs and the Place 1 November are the city's two main squares where political rallies are held. The restaurants and shops nearby make these squares popular for meeting friends.

El Kantara Canyon in the Saharan Atlas Mountains

Little Water

Algeria's only major river is the Chelif, which flows for 450 miles (725 km) from the Atlas Mountains to the Mediterranean Sea. Another important river is the Seybouse. Only the main rivers of the Tell have water year-round. Even there, however, many rivers run dry in the hot summers. The High Plateaus and mountains have some streambeds, but they are dry except in the rainy season. No permanent waterways are found south of the Tell.

Several basins in the High Plateaus collect water during rainy periods, creating large shallow lakes that become salt flats called *chotts* when they dry. The country's lowest point is one of these marshy lake valleys. Chott Melrhir in northeastern Algeria is 102 feet (31 m) below sea level. Its size changes

with the seasons. Throughout most of the year, it is 80 miles (130 km) wide from east to west. Other relatively large Algerian lakes are Sebkha Mekerrhane, Sebkha Azzel-Matti, Chott Merouane, Chott Ech Chergui, and Chott el Hodna. There are also about 170 warm, salty mineral springs, some of which have been used to treat disease since ancient times.

The famous Guelma springs are marked by limestone cones that tower up to 36 feet (11 m) high. The local people call

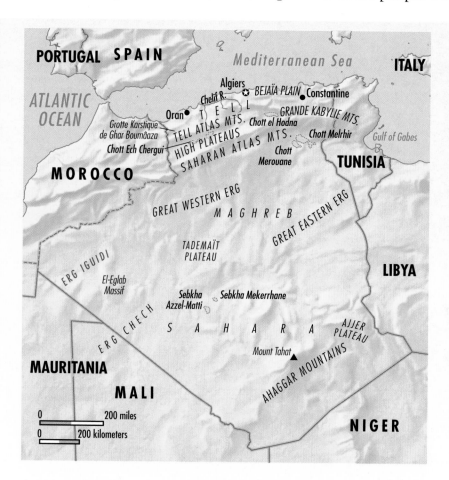

Algeria's Geographical Features

Lowest Elevation: Chott Melrhir, 102 feet (31 m) below sea level

Highest Elevation: Mount Tahat, 9,573 feet (2,918 m)

Average Temperature in Algiers: 77°F (25°C) in July; 53°F (12°C) in January

Average Precipitation: 8 to 16 inches (20 to 40 cm); less than 5 inches (13 cm) in the Sahara

Total Area: 919,595 square miles (2,381,741 sq km)

Distance from East to West: 1,500 miles (2,400 km)

Distance from North to South: 1,300 miles (2,100 km)

Coastline: 750 miles (1,200 km)

the creamy waters Hammam Meskutin, meaning the "cursed baths." A legend says that an ancient tribal leader wanted to marry his beautiful sister. This angered the gods, who sent fire out of the earth to boil their bathwater as the couple was preparing to celebrate the wedding. The man and woman were turned into stone, and their solitary shapes can still be seen.

Sun-baked mud of the Algerian desert

Climate

Temperature varies considerably throughout Algeria, depending on the elevation of the countryside. The Tell region in the north has a typically pleasant Mediterranean climate. The lovely summers are warm and dry, making it perfect for sitting at outdoor cafés and sipping thick, sugary coffee. Winters are generally mild and rainy. This is the most humid area of Algeria, with an annual precipitation ranging from 16 to 39 inches (40 to 100 centimeters). The mean summer and winter temperatures are 77°F (25°C) and 53°F (12°C). Annual precipitation in the High Plateaus and Saharan Atlas ranges from about 8 to 16 inches (20 to 40 cm).

Earthquakes Shake Up the Landscape

Algeria has been shaken by many destructive earthquakes over the years. An earthquake in May 2003 killed twenty-three hundred people and injured more than eleven thousand. More than one hundred twenty thousand people were made homeless, and damage was estimated at $5 billion. On October 10, 1980, the city of El Asnam (now called Ech-Cheliff) was hit by an earthquake that killed at least five thousand people. The same city was also heavily damaged in a 1954 earthquake that killed more than one thousand.

Protecting the Land

Many Algerians are keenly aware of the need to protect their environment. They are trying to protect wetlands that are vital to wildlife and to ensure clean water and air, but the country faces many challenges. Some industries cause pollution by dumping raw sewage or oil refining wastes. Rivers and coastal waters are polluted as soil and fertilizer wash into the waterways. Many people do not have clean water to drink. Overgrazing of animals is hurting the land in some parts of the country. Sand from the desert continually creeps into the more fertile areas. Algerians are working hard to deal with these problems. In 1975, the government began planting a wide barrier of trees south of the Saharan Atlas in an effort to keep the desert sands from drifting northward. This protective green barricade runs for 930 miles (1,500 km).

Wild Algeria

A S IN ALL DESERT COUNTRIES, PATTERNS OF RAINFALL determine what lives in Algeria. The Saharan Atlas Mountains split the country into two easily identifiable regions. North of the mountains, farmers can grow crops without irrigating their fields. South of the mountains, this is impossible.

Opposite: **Brilliant poppies blooming in the spring**

A cork oak stripped of its bark

Hardy Plants

Algeria's plant life is similar to that of southern Europe. Despite the fact that much of Algeria is arid, it still has a wide variety of vegetation— more than 3,100 species, in fact. This includes 162 species found in the Sahara. Towering, fast-growing ash and fragrant cedar are common trees in Algeria. Massive cork oaks grow well in the country's dry soil. Their thick bark is regularly stripped off in large sheets and made into cork for wine bottles, bulletin boards, and other products.

Larger trees include the towering Aleppo pines and the evergreen oak. The jujube produces vitamin-rich berries that are prized as a health

food. Gnarled olive trees grow in thick groves on the rocky hillsides. The Atlantic pinsapo, or Spanish fir, is found on lower mountain slopes. The magnificent date palm, called the King of the Desert, sends its roots deep beneath the Sahara's scattered green oases to reach water. Palm trees can grow to be 120 feet (37 m) tall. The dates they produce are an essential food for Algerians. Harvesters climb the trunk and use forked sticks or ropes to lower the clusters of ripe dates to the ground.

Acacia tree in a scrub desert

Some of Algeria's plants grow quickly after it rains and then retreat to a dormant state. Others, such as athels and acacia, survive with little water. South of the Tell, the landscape is carpeted with hardy esparto grass, which is sometimes used to make high-quality paper for books. Agave, prickly pear, myrtle, and dwarf palm can also be found there. Among the flowers are narcissus, irises, roses, and geraniums.

Algeria's pleasant coastal climate is conducive to growing many varieties of fruits such as dates, pears, nectarines, and peaches. The country's tart lemons, refreshing oranges, chewy figs, sweet plums, and tangy apricots are delicious. Algeria's heavy grapes make excellent red wines. Almonds and tobacco also grow well in Algerian soil.

A genet waiting for prey

Desert Creatures

The north of Algeria has suffered from centuries of deforestation and overgrazing. Projects that help humans survive in the desert have frequently harmed the fragile landscape. For instance, Tourbière du Lac Noir ("the peat bog of the Black Lake") inside El Kala National Park was accidentally drained in 1990 by crews drilling for drinking water and building a road. All that remains of the lake is a bog where yellow water lilies grow. The park is still home to Barbary red deer, Egyptian mongeese, spotted hyenas, and genets—small catlike creatures that feed on mice, insects, and fruit.

A rock painting of hippopotamuses

In ancient days, elephants, hippopotamuses, and even crocodiles lived in Algeria. Rock paintings dating back ten thousand years have been found of these animals, as well as of lions, wild sheep, giraffes, and ostriches. Today, however, the nation's sparse vegetation supports only a limited amount of wildlife. Monkeys, wild boars, porcupines, and hares are plentiful in the country's wilderness regions. Scavengers such as snarling hyenas and rare golden jackals are also found throughout Algeria.

Other large mammals also live in Algeria. The endangered Cuvier's gazelles are good climbers. They make their home amid the rocks and scrub brush of the Atlas Mountains. Today, there are probably about five hundred Cuvier's gazelles left in Algeria and another two thousand in Tunisia and Morocco.

The Perfect Desert Beast

Nomads traditionally used camels to cross the wide deserts, traveling up to 25 miles (40 km) a day at a steady, lumbering pace. The camel remains the symbol of the desert. It can drink up to 30 gallons of water in 10 minutes. Sometimes, camels go weeks without requiring another drink. Well-adapted to the desert, the camel's nostrils and long eyelashes keep out the sand. As camels were domesticated, they changed the history of North Africa. Rather than using oxen-pulled wagons that required roads, desert people developed special saddles that fit atop their camels. They were thus able to roam and raid at will. Today, these humpbacked beasts are slowly being replaced by four-wheel-drive trucks that can haul more cargo.

The Barbary red deer is one of two deer native to Africa. After Europeans colonized North Africa, the animals' habitat rapidly disappeared as trees were cut down and fields were plowed. Today, it is estimated that only about four thousand Barbary red deer remain in Algeria and Tunisia. Barbary sheep, which live in Algeria's arid mountains, are excellent jumpers. They can jump more than 6 feet (2 m) from a standstill.

A common desert creature is the fennec fox. These tiny foxes have huge ears that allow them to hear prey from far

The fennec fox is well-adapted to the Sahara Desert.

away. Fennec foxes stay hidden in the shade of their dens during the day. They come out in the cool of the night to hunt insects, lizards, and other small creatures.

The cheetah, one of the fastest animals on earth, makes its home in the remotest regions of southern Algeria. Like a car in a drag race, it doesn't take long for a sprinting cheetah to hit top speed. The gangly animal can attain 45 miles (72 km) per hour within 2.5 seconds. Its top speed is 70 miles (113 km) per hour for a short run. Long ago, North African royalty trained cheetahs to hunt fleet-footed gazelles.

The Sand Cat

The feisty little sand cat is native to the Sahara Desert. It is perfectly adapted to desert life. The cats have thick pale yellow or gray fur with darker bands, making it easy for them to hide in the desert. The soles of their feet are covered in thick fur that protects them from the desert's hot and cold temperatures. Furry feet also spread the cat's weight so the animal doesn't sink into the sand.

Sand cats come out of their burrows at night to hunt. They hunt silently, with their bellies close to the ground, sometimes reaching speeds of 25 miles (40 km) per hour. They will eat anything they can catch, including gerbils, hamsters, insects, birds, and lizards. One of their favorite snacks is a jerboa, a little desert rodent that hops across the sand and rock like a kangaroo. Because sand cats are excellent diggers, they can go after jerboas in their burrows. They also are great snake hunters. The cats' fast paws hit the snake on the head to stun it. Then the cat kills it by a chomp to the neck.

Algeria is the first landfall after a long, tiring trip across the Mediterranean Sea for birds migrating to Africa from Europe in the spring. Many waterfowl stop in the country's rich salt marshes, where they can feed and rest before continuing their journey. Chott Merouane et Oued Khrouf, 50 miles (80 km) south of Biskra, is one of the most popular resting places. The chott is surrounded by wide stretches of rough sand and low-growing scrub bushes that provide safe nesting for ducks. The lowest part of the chott is permanently flooded with salty water. Flamingos wade across the shallow pools, stirring up mud with their sticklike legs. The birds' large beaks strain

A great flamingo takes flight.

a meal of algae out of the muddy mixture. Common and green-winged teals, pintail ducks, coots, and several varieties of geese are frequently found as well. Birds that prefer land include the woodcock and the Barbary partridge. Algeria is also home to raptors such as golden eagles, hawks, Barbary falcons, and vultures.

The houbara bustard is one of many endangered birds that live in Algeria. This tall bird lives in open, arid areas where it can find seeds and bugs. The northern bald ibis is another species in peril, threatened by climate change, destruction of habitat, pesticide use, and illegal hunting. These magnificent birds stand 2.5 feet (75 cm) tall, with a wingspan of about 4 feet (1.2 m). Their long, narrow beak curves downward, making it easy to forage for food in the marshes. These birds breed only in Morocco, Algeria's neighbor to the west. They fly to Algeria to live in the western Sahara.

Unlike some vultures, Ruppell's griffon vulture is very social, nesting in large colonies of a hundred pairs or more.

The thornback ray has a barbed tail.

Life in Water

The Mediterranean waters off the coast of Algeria teem with life. Sixteen species of sharks can be found in the Mediterranean, including the small-spotted catshark, black-mouth catshark, longnose spurdog, gulper shark, and velvet belly lantern shark. At least five species of large rays live near the Algerian coast, including the starry ray, the thornback ray, and the spotted ray. These fish are often spotted just below the surface of the water, gliding along like oversized butterflies.

Deep in the Sahara, the pools of the Ahaggar National Park are home to interesting fish species such as the desert barbel, a relative of the carp. Fishing for eel is traditional in the Marais de la Mekhada, a freshwater marsh in the reedy Mafragh plain.

Insects and Scorpions

Algeria has a wide range of insects, some of which create problems. The bites of mosquitoes can sometimes transmit a sickness called malaria. In the autumn of 2004, swarms of locusts swept over the Illizi region in the southeast, infesting about 1,000 acres (420 hectares). The insects ate every bit of vegetation they could find. Locusts are considered a delicacy by poor desert people, who cook them in salt water and then let them dry under the hot sun before eating them.

Scorpions thrive in the harsh Algerian landscape. They live underground and come out at night to eat insects, worms, snakes, and rodents. Scorpions, which range in size from 1 to 6 inches (2 to 15 cm) long, have eight legs and two claws, which

A fat-tailed scorpion in El Oued

they use to capture prey. The deadly scorpion is one of the most feared creatures of the desert because of the venom in its spiny tail. Four species of scorpion found in Algeria can kill a person within hours. Algerians, especially those who live in the oases, know to shake out their slippers in the morning and never to reach into a dark corner, for fear of what might be there.

A Legendary Past

HUMANS HAVE LIVED IN NORTH AFRICA FOR AT LEAST forty thousand years. Among the earliest known inhabitants were Berber-speaking nomads. By 3000 B.C., there were some settled Berber groups in what is now Algeria. The landscape was much different then. It had more rainfall and was more fertile. Phoenicians sailed to the region from the eastern end of the Mediterranean and established outposts along the coast in the 1100s B.C. Trade goods flowed out of Africa from their port cities.

Opposite: **A young girl holds a slate of the Qur'an.**

In the 800s B.C., the region that is now Algeria came under the control of the ancient trading city of Carthage, in neighboring Tunisia. By the second century B.C., a Berber chieftain named Massinisa had formed a kingdom called Numidia in northern Algeria. During this period, Rome was frequently at war with Carthage, and Massinisa allied himself with Rome. Massinisa died in 148 B.C. Rome defeated Carthage not long after and then took over Numidia as well in 105 B.C.

A nineteenth-century water-color by Albert Sebille shows a Phoenician trading ship arriving at Alexandria, Egypt.

Roman colonists established farms in the region. Thousands of tons of wheat were exported back to Rome each year, along with figs, grapes, beans, and olive oil. Slaves were also sent to Rome. Over time, the Roman Empire declined. It could no longer protect its far-flung territories. Left defenseless, Algeria came under the control of the Vandals. The Vandals were fierce warriors who stormed out of eastern Germany and made their way across Europe to North Africa. From the Vandals we get the term *vandalize*, which means to wantonly damage something. They controlled much of North Africa from 439 to 534.

Located in the center of North Africa, Algeria was a natural crossroads for invaders. Byzantine troops invaded in 533, defeating the Vandals the following year. In the 600s, Arabs from the Arabian Peninsula to the east invaded the region. They brought with them Islam, a religion established by the prophet Muhammad, which was adopted by most of the Berbers. Many Arabs and Berbers also intermarried. The Rustamid Dynasty, the first Muslim state in Algeria, was established in 777. In the coming centuries, other Muslim dynasties would gain

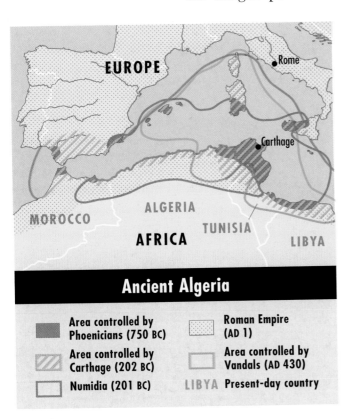

Ancient Algeria

Area controlled by Phoenicians (750 BC)	Roman Empire (AD 1)
Area controlled by Carthage (202 BC)	Area controlled by Vandals (AD 430)
Numidia (201 BC)	LIBYA Present-day country

control, including the Aghlabids, the Fatamids, the Almoravids, and the Almohads.

In the early sixteenth century, Spain captured Algeria's coastal cities, but the Arabs managed to maintain control of the region. The Spanish Christians were finally driven out by Khayr al-Din (ca. 1466–1546), a skilled sea captain who is considered the founder of Algeria. His nickname was Barbarossa, which means "red beard" in Italian. Barbarossa aligned himself with the Ottoman Turks and became their most famous admiral. The Turks retained control of North Africa for the next three hundred years. During this period, the Algerian coast was a stronghold of privateers, or corsairs. Unlike pirates, the corsairs had the permission of the state to seize people and property on its behalf.

A portrait of Barbarossa, the Ottoman's admiral-in-chief

Turkish Rule

The Turks, who were ruled by a sultan, set up an elaborate political system in order to maintain their far-flung territories. Among the local administrators were *pashas*, governors

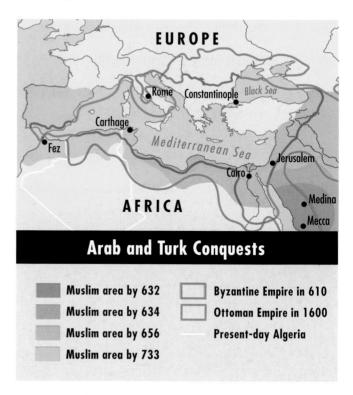

Arab and Turk Conquests

- Muslim area by 632
- Muslim area by 634
- Muslim area by 656
- Muslim area by 733
- Byzantine Empire in 610
- Ottoman Empire in 1600
- Present-day Algeria

A Turkish corsair

who were backed up by a highly trained military force called the *ojaq* in Algeria. These troops were led by an *agha*. After a revolt in 1671, the ojaq killed their agha and named their own commander, called the *dey*. Supposedly installed for life, the position of dey was not very secure. Over the next one hundred fifty years, fourteen deys were assassinated in power struggles.

Slave trading was a significant part of the Algerian economy during this era. Corsairs captured ships and sold the lower-class travelers as laborers. More important captives were ransomed. Sailors, blacksmiths, and carpenters were especially prized because of their skills. Some slaves were treated very well, and a few even inherited a great deal of wealth when their masters died. Others were ill fed and worked almost to death in stone quarries or on farms. There was some hope for prisoners, however. Priests raised money throughout Europe and journeyed to Algeria to purchase as many captives as they could. The deys received this money eagerly and treated the priests with respect.

After all, the slave trade was merely a matter of economics in the minds of those who were involved at this time.

Some historians say that at least four hundred thousand Christians were sold in the sprawling Algiers slave market between 1520 and 1660. But it must also be remembered that captured Muslims were enslaved in Spain, Malta, Italy, France, and other European countries. If a captured Christian became a Muslim and later was freed, he often would be put to death instead of being welcomed back home. In Europe, it was considered a sin to change religions, regardless of the reason.

Corsairs attack the English warship *Triton*.

Some Europeans freely offered their services as corsairs to the deys because of the status and money they could earn in North Africa. Many of these Europeans converted to Islam. They often lived very well if they had talents as soldiers or ship captains. These men were considered outlaws and pirates by their home nations.

Many nations paid tribute money to the corsairs and the dey so that their ships would not be attacked. Even the young United States sent tribute to the dey, including a 36-gun frigate ship delivered in 1798. In 1812, a disagreement over tribute led the dey to declare war on the United States. In 1815, an American fleet commanded by Stephen Decatur sailed into the Mediterranean. The Americans killed the most famous corsair, Hamidou Rais, and captured his frigate. A treaty ending the hostilities was soon signed. This battle, along with the bombarding of Algiers by the British and the Dutch in 1816, weakened the power of the dey.

Commodore Stephen Decatur, U.S. naval commander

The French Invasion

In the 1820s, France was also in turmoil. The French king, Charles X, was unpopular, and the French soon took advantage of events in Algeria to distract people from the problems at home. In 1827, the dey and a French diplomat got into an argument because the French were refusing to pay their debts. The dey swatted the diplomat with a fly whisk. The insult gave the French an excuse to blockade Algeria. They invaded Algiers three years later.

Algeria officially became part of France in 1848, after the French crushed a bloody revolt led by Abd al-Qadir (1807–1883). Al-Qadir was a popular Muslim leader who had declared a holy war against the invaders and is still revered by the Algerians for his bravery and statesmanship. With peace, some Europeans moved to Algeria. The French gave many of them, called *colons*, large tracts of land. The native Muslim population had little political or economic power.

Abd al-Qadir led the struggle against French domination in the 1830s and 1840s.

A Legendary Past **45**

The Algerians fought with the French from 1914 to 1918 during World War I. At the war's end, however, a strong nationalist movement developed. Algeria was a battleground during World War II, when the Allies—Britain, the United States, France, and many other countries—were fighting the aggression of Germany and Italy. The French surrendered to Nazi Germany in 1940. The French leaders who agreed to work with the Germans formed a puppet government based in the city of Vichy, France. Vichy officials also ran Algeria.

Meanwhile, Free French troops, including Algerians, continued to resist the Germans. In 1942, British, American, and Free French troops invaded Algeria. Algiers became the headquarters of the Allied forces in the fight for North Africa as well as the home of the Free French government led by General Charles de Gaulle. The chief of the Allied forces was American general Dwight D. Eisenhower, who lived in Algeria for six months. Eisenhower's office can still be seen in the historic Hotel Al-Djaza'ir in Algiers.

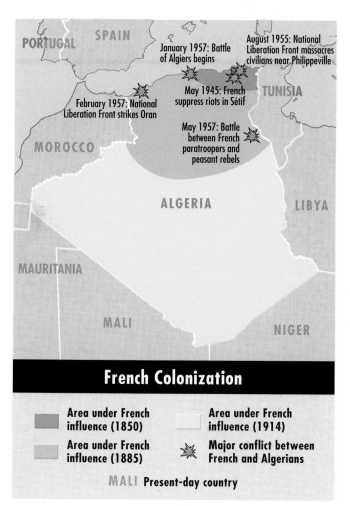

French Colonization

- Area under French influence (1850)
- Area under French influence (1885)
- Area under French influence (1914)
- Major conflict between French and Algerians
- MALI Present-day country

January 1957: Battle of Algiers begins

August 1955: National Liberation Front massacres civilians near Philippeville

February 1957: National Liberation Front strikes Oran

May 1945: French suppress riots in Sétif

May 1957: Battle between French paratroopers and peasant rebels

The Allies won the war in 1945. After the war, Algerians continued their quest for independence. The colons were afraid of losing control of Algeria, and they refused to make any political reforms that might have eased the tension. A revolt led by the Algerian National Liberation Front (FLN) broke out in 1954 and continued for seven years. The French faced ambushes, bombings, and assassinations, and they were ruthless in fighting back. Orchards and farm fields were destroyed, homes were burned, and people were tortured. The French public back home began to object to the rough methods used

Riot police throw tear gas bombs and stones at demonstrators on December 10, 1960, in the city of Algiers.

Capturing the Revolution

Italian director Gillo Pontecorvo's noted 1965 movie, *The Battle of Algiers*, dealt with the violent struggle for Algerian independence from France. The film's message was so powerful that the film was banned in France for a time because the government feared it would result in riots. *The Battle of Algiers* was shot as a documentary, using untrained actors. Pontecorvo graphically and sympathetically showed how the war affected the colonists and the soldiers. Considered one of the finest movies of its type ever made, *The Battle of Algiers* was the forerunner of other such movies that had a real-life feel to them. Prior to the U.S. invasion of Iraq in 2003, Defense Department officials studied the film to learn about fighting an urban war against determined insurgents. The movie was re-released to great acclaim in American theaters in 2004.

to battle the rebellion. More than five hundred thousand people took part in an antiwar demonstration in 1962.

Finally, the French government decided enough was enough and granted Algeria its much-awaited independence on July 3, 1962. Most of the colons soon fled the country and returned to France. Tens of thousands of Algerians, French soldiers and officials, and colons had been killed over the course of the revolution.

Ben Bella Becomes President

Revolutionary leader Ahmed Ben Bella, a former Free French soldier, became president of Algeria after independence. He supported state control of business and industry and encouraged Algeria's poor to take over the farms abandoned by the colons. Ben Bella was deposed by army commander Houari Boumedienne in 1965. Boumedienne led the country until his death in 1978. Even more than Ben Bella, he was committed to having the government control the economy. To this end, the Algerian government took over the French oil interests in the Sahara in 1971. Boumedienne also worked to rapidly increase the amount of industry in Algeria. When Boumedienne died, he was succeeded by Chadli Benjedid, who reduced the government's role in the economy.

Algeria's first president, Ahmed Ben Bella, delivers an address to the Algerian National Assembly.

Rebellion

By the mid-1980s, the economy was in a sharp downturn, and people were angry at the government, which was seen as corrupt. In 1988, riots swept across the country. In the aftermath of those riots, government and society became freer. Previously, the FLN had been the only political party allowed in Algeria. But a change in the constitution in 1989 allowed other parties to arise. Parliamentary elections were held in December 1991, and the Islamic Salvation Front, known as FIS, won 44 percent of the seats. A second round of elections was to be

A 1997 demonstration against violence

held in January, and it was likely that the FIS would win a majority of the seats in parliament. People feared that Algeria was on its way to becoming an Islamic state. To head this off, the army forced Benjedid to resign, and the election results were set aside. A governing council dominated by the military was put in charge of Algeria. The Islamic party was also outlawed and many of its members arrested, causing the outbreak of another rebellion. By the end of the 1990s, this civil unrest had caused an estimated one hundred fifty thousand deaths. Thousands of people fled to France to escape the bloodshed and to find greater economic freedom.

General Liamine Zéroual, who was appointed president in 1994,

President Liamine Zéroual

attempted to negotiate a peace settlement but failed. In 1999, he was replaced by Abdelaziz Bouteflika, who was favored by the military, in an election that some people said was rife with fraud. Islamist rebels continued to wage war against the Algerian government. In 2005, Algerians voted in favor of pardoning both military forces and rebels for most crimes committed during the unrest. They hope that this will help end a bloody chapter in the nation's history.

How Government Functions

ALGERIA'S OFFICIAL NAME IS THE PEOPLE'S DEMOcratic Republic of Algeria. The country's current constitution was adopted on November 19, 1976. Since then, it has undergone revisions in 1988, 1989, and 1996.

Algeria is divided into forty-eight *wilayas*, which are like states or provinces. They are headed by *walis* (governors) who report to the Minister of Interior. Each wilaya is divided into communes, the basic units of government. The wilayas are governed by locally elected assemblies.

Opposite: **President Abdelaziz Bouteflika**

A boy helps his father vote in a recent election.

The Algerian Constitution says that political parties are free to operate, but they must have the permission of the Ministry of Interior. After the Islamic Salvation Front almost took control of the government, the constitution was changed to outlaw parties formed on the basis of religion, language, race, gender, or region.

Today, between forty and fifty political parties are operating in Algeria. They are all eager to make their voices heard in local and national elections. Among the most prominent are the National Liberation Front, the National Democratic Rally, the Movement for National Reform, the Movement of the Society for Peace, the Socialist Forces Front, and the Rally for Culture and Democracy.

An Islamic Salvation Front leader, Ali Benhadj, is released from jail.

"Dandy" Bouteflika Becomes President

Algeria's president, Abdelaziz Bouteflika, took office in April 1999. He was reelected in April 2004, with 84 percent of the vote. Bouteflika was born March 2, 1937, in Morocco near his family's hometown of Tlemcen, in western Algeria. As a young man, Bouteflika was an officer in the National Liberation Army fighting against French rule. When Algeria first gained independence, Bouteflika was Algeria's minister of youth, sport, and tourism. At age twenty-six, he became foreign minister, a position he held from 1963 to 1979. His negotiating skills were highly regarded, especially after he made agreements with the French regarding oil interests in Algeria. In 1981, Bouteflika left Algeria after being charged with corruption. He lived in exile in France and Switzerland until the charges were dropped.

With the support of the army, Bouteflika ran for the Algerian presidency in 1999. He was elected with 73 percent of the vote, but all the other candidates had withdrawn because they were certain the election was fixed. Although the election was criticized both in Algeria and around the world, Bouteflika remained in office.

Civil strife was raging when Bouteflika took office, and he made restoring peace and security central to his presidency. He promoted a harmony policy that provided amnesty, or pardon, to large numbers of the

Islamic Salvation Army who were fighting against the government.

Bouteflika is considered upper class and oriented toward Western-style politics. His nickname, the Dandy Diplomat, is a result of his well-tailored clothes and refined manner of speech.

Branches of Government

The Algerian government is divided into three branches. The executive branch is led by the president, who is elected directly by the people to a five-year term. The president can run for a second term. To be a candidate for president, a

Prime Minister Ahmed Ouyahia

person must be forty years old, a Muslim, and of Algerian nationality. The candidate's spouse must also be Algerian.

The president has many duties. He is the head of all the armed forces and is responsible for national defense. He directs the country's foreign policy and concludes treaties. The president chairs the Council of Ministers and names the prime minister—and can remove that person from office. He also appoints the president of the Council of State, the secretary general of the government, and the governor of the Bank of Algeria, as well as magistrates and the walis.

The head of government is the prime minister, who is appointed by the president. Ahmed Ouyahia has held the job since May 2003. The prime minister signs executive decrees and oversees the various operations of government. The National Assembly exerts a lot of influence on what the prime minister does. If the assembly does not support what the prime minister is doing, he must resign, and the president then names a new prime minister.

A cabinet called the Council of Ministers takes care of the day-to-day running of the government. They oversee departments such as the Interior Ministry, the Ministry for Youth and Sports, the Ministry for Finance, the Ministry for Energy and the Mines, and the Ministry for Foreign Affairs.

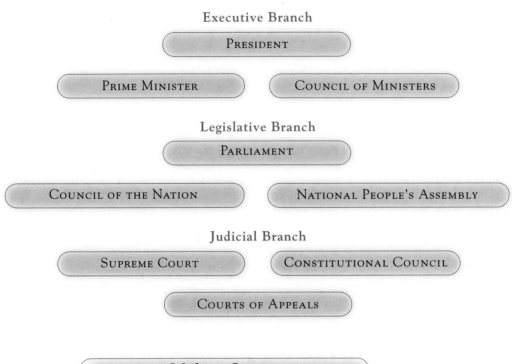

NATIONAL GOVERNMENT OF ALGERIA

Executive Branch

PRESIDENT

PRIME MINISTER

COUNCIL OF MINISTERS

Legislative Branch

PARLIAMENT

COUNCIL OF THE NATION

NATIONAL PEOPLE'S ASSEMBLY

Judicial Branch

SUPREME COURT

CONSTITUTIONAL COUNCIL

COURTS OF APPEALS

Making Laws

Algeria's legislative branch is a two-house parliament. It consists of the National People's Assembly, which has 389 seats. Members, who are elected by popular vote, serve five-year terms. The other house of parliament is a senate called the Council of the Nation, with 144 seats. One-third of these members are appointed by the president. The remaining two-thirds are elected by regional and municipal authorities. Members of the Council of the Nation serve six-year terms.

The president, the Council of the Nation, and the assembly all have the authority to initiate legislation. Any law being considered must be approved by both chambers of parliament

before it goes into effect. Algerians are very interested in watching their government in action, and sessions of parliament are televised.

The Legal System

Abdelaziz Belkhadem, Algeria's foreign minister, addresses the United Nations in 2001.

Algeria's legal system is based on a combination of French and Islamic law. The Supreme Court is the country's highest judicial body. There are two levels of appeals courts. One

Algeria's Flag Flies High

Algeria's flag was adopted after independence in 1962. On one half of the flag is a vertical band of green. On the other half is a vertical band of white. In the middle is a red, five-pointed star within a red crescent. These are the traditional symbols of Islam, the state religion. Green stands for Islam, while white indicates purity. According to some historians, white is also a reminder of Algerian revolutionary leader Abd al-Qadir, who used a white flag while fighting the French in 1847. The flag was adopted by Algeria's National Liberation Front in 1954. It was based on a

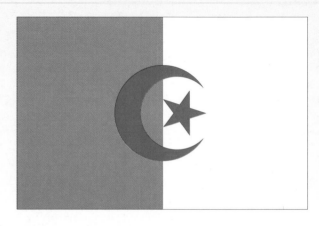

design dating from 1928 that had been used by the nationalist leader Messali Hadj.

attends to civil matters involving lawsuits, property disputes, and related issues. The other is a nationwide system of Courts of Appeals that review decisions by lower courts. Another government authority is the Constitutional Council, which has nine members. This council rules on the constitutionality of treaties and related international issues.

International Affairs

Algeria plays an important role in international affairs and lends its voice to Islamic causes, as well as supporting other African nations. Algeria belongs to the United Nations, the World Trade Organization, the International Maritime Organization, and many other associations that promote issues such as environmental protection and nuclear disarmament. It is also very active in the Organization of Petroleum Exporting Countries (OPEC).

The National Anthem

The Algerian national anthem, "Qassaman" ("We Swear"), was adopted in 1963. The words are by Mufdi Zakariah, and the music is by Mohamed Fawzi.

We swear by the lightning that destroys,
By the streams of generous blood being shed,
By the bright flags that wave,
Flying proudly on the high mountains,
That we are in revolt, whether to live or to die,
We are determined that Algeria should live,
So be our witness—be our witness—be our witness!

We are soldiers in revolt for truth
And we have fought for our independence.
When we spoke, nobody listened to us,
So we have taken the noise of gunpowder as our rhythm
And the sound of machine guns as our melody,
We are determined that Algeria should live,
So be our witness—be our witness—be our witness!

From our heroes we shall make an army come to being,
From our dead we shall build up a glory,
Our spirits shall ascend to immortality
And on our shoulders we shall raise the Standard.
To the nation's Liberation Front we have sworn an oath,
We are determined that Algeria should live,
So be our witness—be our witness—be our witness!

The cry of the Fatherland sounds from the battlefields.
Listen to it and answer the call!
Let it be written with the blood of martyrs
And be read to future generations.
Oh, Glory, we have held out our hand to you,
We are determined that Algeria should live,
So be our witness—be our witness—be our witness!

The People's National Army, Algerian National Navy, Algerian Air Force, and Territorial Air Defense Force are responsible for defending Algeria. At age nineteen, Algerian men are required to do military service for eighteen months. The military plays a strong role in Algerian politics. Officers, particularly in the army, are often outspoken about political issues.

Algeria was born in revolution. It has faced many internal political challenges, and today it continues to solidify its leadership role on the world stage.

A soldier patrols the streets of Algiers.

Algiers: Did You Know This?

Algiers is Algeria's capital and largest city, with 1,886,000 residents. The nation's primary commercial city, Algiers has quadrupled in population since the 1950s.

Algiers began as a fort on a high hill overlooking the Mediterranean. It is an ancient city, with Phoenician traders arriving as early as the 1100s B.C. Their ships found a good harbor in the Bay of Algiers, as did subsequent waves of occupiers such as the Carthaginians, Romans, Arabs, and Turks.

The oldest part of town, known as the casbah, is a jumble of homes and tiny storefronts. The neighborhood's steep stairways leading up and down the bluff are packed with people going about their daily business. White office buildings and warehouses pile along to the waterfront, where ships from many nations dock to load and unload cargo.

Algiers is a colorful mishmash of architectural styles. One of its most notable structures is the 330-foot-tall (100-m) Martyr's Monument, located in a large square about 1.8 miles (3 km) from the center of the city. Sailors use the towering monument as a navigational aid. Many of Algiers's beautiful old religious buildings,

such as the mosque of Djemaa el Djedid, are also well preserved.

Algiers's coastal location makes its climate pleasant. Temperatures range from about 53°F (12°C) in January to about 77°F (25°C) in June.

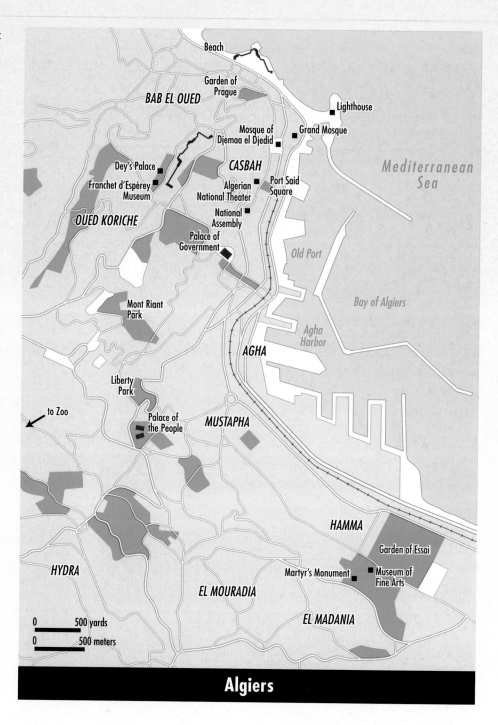

Algiers

A Nation of Oil

S HEETS OF ALMOST WHITE-HOT HEAT COOK THE SAHARA Desert, even while snow caps the distant mountains. A large four-wheel-drive truck carrying sweating technicians bounces over a rough trail leading to a remote oil field. To get over the dunes, the driver attacks the sandy slope by gunning the engine to full throttle. Grunting, the truck jumps ahead, reaching the crest of the dune and sliding down the far side. The men inside the vehicle scan the harsh Algerian scenery from behind their sunglasses. The sun's glare is a blazing heat lamp.

It is a relief once the far-off tents and low huts surrounding the oil-drilling equipment are finally spotted. When the men arrive in the camp, they eagerly gulp cold drinks and wolf down a hearty meal before changing clothes and heading to work.

Opposite: **Oil refinery at Skikda**

Oil drilling in Hassi Messaoud

Large Reserves of Oil and Gas

Algeria's desert environment is challenging. Yet beneath the inhospitable surface lie large reserves of oil and natural gas. These resources are the mainstays of the economy, accounting for roughly 60 percent of budget revenues, 30 percent of gross domestic product, and more than 95 percent of export earnings. Signs of the oil industry are everywhere. The country abounds with derricks above wells, pipelines that snake for miles, cloud-snagging smokestacks at refineries, and rotund storage tanks.

Gas is burned off at an oil refinery in Hassi Messaoud.

In 1956, oil was first discovered in central Algeria's vast Hassi Messaoud oil field. The industry has been expanding in Algeria ever since. The nation hopes to be producing two million barrels of crude oil per day by 2010.

Sonatrach, Algeria's national oil company, operates all the major oil fields. Algeria partners with exploration firms and investors from at least forty different nations to open new oil fields. Among them are the Halliburton and Anadarko companies from the United States, Brazil's Petrobras, British Petroleum, TotalFinaElf from France, Enagas and Repsol from Spain, Statoil from Norway, and the Kuwait Foreign Petroleum Exploration Company. Fifty-four wells were drilled during 2004, up from forty-three in 2003 and twenty-nine in 2002.

Pipes carry oil at a refinery built with funds from outside investors.

OPEC's representatives meet in Algiers.

Almost 90 percent of Algeria's oil exports go to western Europe. Italy is the main market, followed by Germany, France, the Netherlands, Spain, and Britain. They all want Algeria's Saharan Blend oil, which is among the highest quality petroleum in the world.

Algeria also has the world's fifth-largest reserves of natural gas and is the world's second-largest gas exporter. The

Controlling the Oil Supply

Algeria belongs to the powerful Organization of Petroleum Exporting Countries (OPEC). OPEC's eleven member nations supply about 40 percent of the world's oil and control more than three-quarters of the world's total reserves. OPEC works hard to stabilize the oil market by adjusting the oil output to be sure there is always a balance between supply and demand. If too much oil is produced, prices drop. At least twice a year, the oil and energy ministers of member states meet to decide on their output level. OPEC's mission is to make sure that all member nations benefit equally.

Hassi R'Mel gas field, discovered in 1956 south of Algiers, holds one of the country's largest reserves. About 7.5 billion cubic yards (5.7 billion cubic meters) of natural gas was exported in 2001. Algeria's goal is to export at least three trillion cubic feet per year by 2010. Algeria has two major gas pipelines to Europe, one to Italy, and one to Spain. It is currently building a second pipeline to Spain under the Mediterranean.

Mineral Wealth

Besides oil and gas, Algeria also has other resources under the ground. Iron, lead, zinc, copper, calamine, antimony, mercury, and lignite coal are all mined in Algeria. Extensive phosphate beds were discovered near Tebessa in 1891. Phosphate, which is used in fertilizer and other products, is still being mined today. The collection of salt along the edges of the chotts is another profitable business for Algeria. More than three hundred quarries provide valuable stones such as onyx and white and red marble. The ancient Romans used Algerian onyx mined by slaves in Ain Tekbalet. The remains of ancient quarries have been discovered near Kleber.

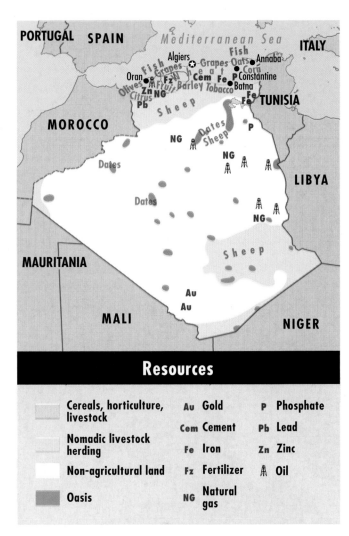

Resources

Cereals, horticulture, livestock	Au Gold	P Phosphate
Nomadic livestock herding	Cem Cement	Pb Lead
Non-agricultural land	Fe Iron	Zn Zinc
	Fz Fertilizer	⚒ Oil
Oasis	NG Natural gas	

Factories, Farms, and Fish

Before independence, the major manufactured products in Algeria were processed foods, textiles, and clothing. Today, iron, steel, textiles, and construction materials are the major products. Industries such as electrical firms, food processing, and construction are mainstays of the Algerian economy. About 32 percent of the population works for the government in one way or another.

Agriculture accounts for 10 percent of the economic production and provides jobs for about 14 percent of Algeria's workers. They grow cereals such as rye, barley, and oats, plus fruits such as figs, grapes, and olives.

Tuaregs harvest barley and wheat near Illamane.

What Algeria Grows, Makes, and Mines

Agriculture (2003)

Wheat	3.55 million metric tons
Barley	1.5 million metric tons
Corn	3.048 million metric tons

Manufacturing

Cement (2002)	2,003,000 metric tons
Steel (2003)	266,000 metric tons

Mining

Oil (2004)	11.87 million barrels/day
Natural gas (2001)	80 billion cubic meters/day
Gold (2003)	365 kilograms

More than 7,500,000 acres (3,000,000 ha) in the Tell are used to grow grains. A small amount of cotton is also grown in the southern oases where there is little soil to be cultivated. Innovative Algerians find remarkable uses for just about anything growing in their country. They strip a tough fiber known as vegetable horse-hair from the leaves of the dwarf palm. The greenish strands are dried and then twisted and sold in large bundles to factories that make furniture and mattress stuffing, ropes, and baskets. Tobacco is also successfully cultivated. Sheep are raised for their wool and meat, while cattle are raised for dairy products and meat.

Fishing is a small but important segment of the economy. Blue and red shrimp and deep-water pink shrimp are found in the Mediterranean waters, as are sardines, bonito, smelt, and

A fishmonger at the market in Boufarik

sprats. Striped red mullet and sea bream make delicious stews and fish pies, while tasty sardines and anchovies are caught for the snack market. About 84 percent of Algeria's fresh and preserved fish catch is shipped to Spain, with the remainder going to France and Italy.

After breaking from France, Algeria began playing a major role in planning its economy. The government took control of many industries. It worked to industrialize the economy, putting a lot of money into the construction of factories. By the 1980s, however, there was less central government planning in the economy. In 1994, a law permitted the privatization of some state-owned companies. The state subsequently sold a cement factory and put other industries up for sale to private buyers. Today, most small factories are privately owned. The government is hoping that banking reforms, along with encouraging investments and reducing government bureaucracy, will improve Algeria's business climate.

An Algerian woman learns skills that will enable her to run a home business.

Algeria continues to face serious economic problems. One of the greatest challenges is high unemployment. Government officials say that 25 percent of Algerians were out of work in 2004, but outside observers say that number could be much higher. Some people believe that 50 percent of Algerians under thirty years old do not have regular jobs. In the large cities, groups of unemployed young men, the *haitists* (meaning the "people who prop up walls"), lounge around the cafés and on street corners.

Algerian Money

The basic unit of Algerian currency is the Algerian dinar. It is divided into 100 centimes. In August 2005, 73 dinars equaled 1 U.S. dollar. Algeria issues coins in denominations of 5, 10, 20, and 50 centimes and 1, 5, and 10 dinars. There are also banknotes in denominations of 5, 10, 20, 50, 100, 200, 500, and 1,000 dinars. The banknotes are very colorful. A thirteenth-century corsair warship adorns the blue 100-dinar note. The 200-dinar note has pictures of the Martyr's Monument.

Many Algerians read papers to keep up with the news.

Keeping in Touch

Young Algerians, like their counterparts in the rest of the world, love talking on the telephone. There are relatively few phones in the country, however—probably not more than five per one hundred persons. Algeria has twenty-five AM radio stations and one FM outlet, as well as forty-six television stations. Internet is just starting, with an estimated five hundred thousand users.

Keeping up with the news is considered very important in Algeria. The country has more than thirty daily newspapers. Some, such as *El Watan*, are published in French, while others, such as *El Khabar*, are in Arabic. No English-language newspapers are published in Algeria, but copies of the *International Herald Tribune* are usually available at hotel newsstands. While journalists are generally free to write what they wish, they need to be careful. Being too critical of the government can sometimes get them into trouble. As one means of keeping the media in check, the government has total control over the distribution of newsprint.

An Algerian rush hour

To get goods to and from the market, and to transport people from one place to another, Algeria has 2,469 miles (3,973 km) of railroad tracks and 64,622 miles (104,000 km) of roads. In the Sahara, the Algerian government has classified roads by degree of risk, ranging from not risky to very dangerous. Motorists wishing to take certain roads must get permission from the local authorities, who check the drivers' vehicles to ensure they meet safety standards. The desert is an unforgiving place if there is a breakdown. Some places in the desert sport signs that warn of wandering camels, much like the deer alert signs on U.S. highways.

True to its seafaring heritage, Algeria still has many bust-ling ports that serve oceangoing vessels. International airports are located at Algiers, Constantine, Annaba, and Oran. The country is served by Air Algérie, Royal Air Maroc, Tunis Air, EgyptAir, Air France, and other airlines. They ensure that ideas, as well as goods, keep flowing in and out of Algeria.

The Port of Algiers

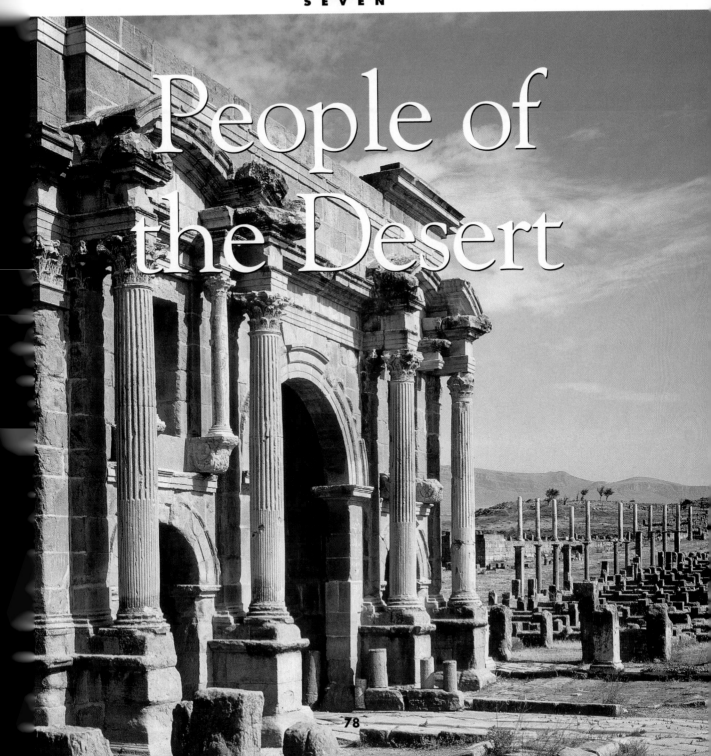

People of the Desert

Most of North Africa was once much more fertile than it is now. Perhaps a half million years ago, the first humans traveled across the woodlands and savannah that once existed here. People found food in the forests and hunted the plentiful game. Prehistoric art from between 8,000 and 5,500 B.C. has been found in caves and on canyon walls in many parts of the country. More than four hundred thousand drawings of animals, hunters, and herders adorn the rocks on the Tassili N'Ajjer, east of Djanet. A more remote site at Tadart also has ancient paintings.

The earliest known inhabitants of what is now Algeria were the Berbers. When North Africa was fertile, they used horses to get around. Then, in about 2,000 B.C., the climate of

Opposite: **Triumphal arch of the Roman emperor Trajan**

Prehistoric rock carvings near Djanet

North Africa began to change. Drought parched the land, forcing a change in the lifestyle of the people. They needed to dig deeper wells or to move in search of fresh water. The large animals that they had hunted migrated south to more lush areas of central Africa. The desert sands began overtaking the land. The Berbers gave up their horses. Instead, they domesticated camels, strange-looking animals better suited to the desert environment.

A camel caravan in the Sahara Desert

Arabs arrived in Algeria from the east in the late 600s. They brought with them the religion of Islam. The new religion, along with the Arabic language and culture, caused major cultural changes that eventually affected all of North Africa.

Over the centuries, Arabs and Berbers intermingled. Today, only a small minority identify themselves as totally Berber, and they live in the rugged, mountainous Kabylie region to the east of Algiers. Though they are Muslim, they emphasize their Berber heritage and have sought more political freedom from Algerian rule. Such independence will not happen in the near future, but the government has promised to begin teaching the Berber language in schools and has encouraged Berber arts and literature.

Berber women

Berber Peoples

The Tuaregs, a Berber people, have made their homes in the central Sahara for at least thirty-five hundred years. Long ago, they learned to adapt to the harsh climate, dust storms, lack of water, and searing heat. They followed their herds of animals that moved among tiny islands of green in the sea of sand and rock. Despite these challenges, there was an advantage to living in this remote backland, one that would make the Tuaregs rich, powerful, and feared.

The Sahara lay between the riches of central Africa and the seacoast markets. Traders crossed the desert in caravans of more than one thousand camels laden with goods. These slow camel trains traveled north across the desert, bearing gold, slaves, salt, ivory, grain, and even bundles of live chickens. Returning south, the caravans were loaded with beads, cloth, and other trade goods. The Tuaregs took advantage of the traders' long, lonely trek, roaming the desert in search of loot. They rode fighting camels, which they had bred to have long, low bodies for speed and agility. The Tuaregs exacted tolls from the caravans in exchange for safe passage, or they simply took what they wanted. In the 1800s, the French sent troops to end the

A nomadic Tuareg painted by S. M. Durban

Tuaregs' desert piracy. Only when the French sent in highly mobile soldiers who fought the Tuareg way were the raids stopped. Brutal repression of the Tuaregs followed.

These days, many Tuaregs are giving up their nomadic ways and settling down. Camels are giving way to trucks. But Tuareg men still often wear the blue protective face scarves and long robes that earned them the nickname the Blue Men.

Other Berber groups are the fiercely independent Kabyles who live in the Kabylie mountains, the Chaouia of the Aurès mountains, and the M'zab. The M'zab established five cities in a valley in the western Sahara a thousand years ago. Each town is on a hill that is topped by a mosque. More than three thousand wells support the M'zab communities, which are linked by tens of thousands of palm trees. Today, these desert towns of stone houses are home to three hundred sixty thousand people. The M'zab are also noted merchants, with shops in Algiers and France.

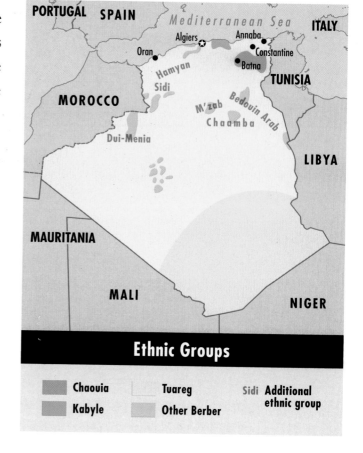

Ethnic Groups

Chaouia	Tuareg	Sidi Additional ethnic group
Kabyle	Other Berber	

Europeans

More than one million Europeans, primarily from France, lived in Algeria before independence in 1962. More than

Ethnic Population of Algeria

Arab or Arab-Berber mix	83%
Berber	16%
European	1%

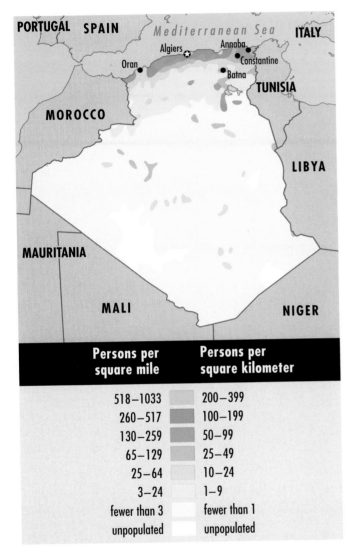

Persons per square mile	Persons per square kilometer
518–1033	200–399
260–517	100–199
130–259	50–99
65–129	25–49
25–64	10–24
3–24	1–9
fewer than 3	fewer than 1
unpopulated	unpopulated

Population of Algeria's Major Cities

Algiers	1,886,000
Oran	1,110,000
Constantine	808,000

90 percent of them left after the successful revolution. Now Europeans make up less than 1 percent of the citizenry. In addition to the few remaining French are Italians and Spaniards and a number of people from the Mediterranean islands of Malta and Corsica.

Life in Algeria

As of 2005, Algeria had an estimated population of 32,531,853. It is a very young country—about three-quarters of the population is under thirty years old. Almost 30 percent are fourteen years old and under. The average life span for a man is seventy-one years, while a woman can usually count on living to at least seventy-four years of age.

About 90 percent of Algerians live in the Tell, the fertile flatland near the Mediterranean. Outside the northern cities, the population is more spread out, with an average of about 36 people per square mile (14 people per sq km). In the cities, men work in offices and factories. In the country, most are farmers or laborers. Civil servants and soldiers staff the hot, dusty frontier outposts far from the com-

forts of Algiers. Many rural families, however, have moved to the cities in search of work. Since there are not enough jobs, this has created a ring of slums around most larger Algerian towns, especially those along the coast.

In rural communities, Algerians often wear loose-fitting traditional clothing because it is comfortable and cool. A woman wears a long outer garment called a *haik*, while a man usually wears a hooded cloak called a *burnoose*. Many city residents wear Western-style clothes. T-shirts, jeans, and tennis shoes are popular. Girls often cover their heads with scarves.

Algerian girls wear both Western and traditional clothing.

Arabic, the official language of Algeria, is spoken by approximately 83 percent of the people. Many people also speak French, while English is often used in the international business community. About 14 percent of the Berbers, most of whom live in the northern mountains, still speak a Berber dialect. For instance, the Tuaregs speak the Berber dialect Tamahaq, though some may also speak Arabic.

There is often tension between Arabic-speaking and Berber-speaking Algerians. After independence, Algeria's new leaders promoted the use of Arabic rather than French in schools and throughout society. In many cases, only Arabic

Two elderly gentlemen converse in Ghardaia.

A book in Arabic is read from right to left.

was allowed to be used. Many Berbers objected to this. In 2001, a young Berber man was killed while in police custody. This led to violent protests in which 125 people were killed. In the aftermath of this unrest, the government dropped the Arabic-only policy. Today, Tamazight, a Berber tongue, is recognized as a national language, though it is not yet an "official" language. Many Berbers continue to speak French to show their opposition to Arabic.

Arabic is the sacred language of Islam. It is spoken across North Africa and throughout the Middle East. It is used on television and radio and in books, official documents, newspapers, and magazines. In school, children learn to read in Arabic, a language in which the writing flows from right to left. There are many dialects of Arabic. Words with Arabic roots are found in Italian and Spanish because the Arabs ruled parts of those countries long ago. A number of English words can also be traced to Arabic, including algebra, mosque, and sultan.

Algerian teachers work hard to promote literacy in schools. The literacy rate has greatly improved since Algeria gained independence.

Algerians have a great love of learning. Schools are valued. Before independence, most teachers came from France. All classes were taught in French, with Arabic offered only as a second language. After independence, the government changed the system to emphasize Arabic language and customs. Teachers worked hard to promote literacy (the ability to read and write). Although the literacy rate was less than 10 percent in 1962, by 1990 more half the population could read. Today, 70 percent of Algerians age fifteen or over are literate.

In the 1970s, the government took control of all schools and no longer allowed private schools. School is free from the first grade all the way through university. Today, young

people between the ages of six and fifteen must go to classes, most of which are taught by Algerians. The children learn Arabic during the first nine years of school. French can be taken in the third year and is the usual language for teaching advanced math and science. English, Spanish, or Italian can also be studied in the higher grades. Children learn to write in Western script and traditional, flowing Arabic script. Arabic calligraphy is a major art form, and skilled practitioners are highly regarded.

A child practices writing Western script.

After nine years of elementary school, students may go on to a *lycée*, or secondary school. At the lycées, there are both general and technical programs in science, mathematics, and other subjects. During their third year of lycée, students take a difficult exam to qualify for graduation. Passing this test allows students to go on to higher education. Some youngsters who do not attend a lycée go to a vocational school, where they can learn a trade. The vocational school system offers five-year apprenticeship programs to prepare young people for work in factories or on farms.

Because the majority of Algerians are under the age of twenty, schools are strained. In some city schools, children go to class in shifts. One group attends in the morning, and a second group goes in the afternoon. It is also difficult to provide schooling for students living far from the populated coastal area. In the desert regions, where there are only a few villages and far-flung military outposts, it is hard to maintain schools.

About three hundred fifty thousand Algerians are in college at any given time. Algeria is proud of its universities. The largest is the University of Algiers, which was started as a medical school in 1859. The university has a strong international mindset and maintains exchange programs linking it to the world. The University of Oran, the University of Constantine, and the University of Science and Technology of Algiers are other major Algerian universities.

CHAPTER

EIGHT

There Is Only One God

I N ANCIENT NORTH AFRICA, MANY PEOPLE WERE PAGANS who worshipped a variety of gods and goddesses, or the earth, sun, and other objects from nature. Each conquering culture—whether from Carthage, Rome, or elsewhere—layered its own religious practices on the region. Christianity gained a foothold along the Mediterranean coast in the years following the death of Jesus. Christian church fathers such as Augustine of Hippo, Origen and Clement of Alexandria, and Tertullian and Cyprian of Carthage are the best known of the North African religious leaders from this era.

It was Islam that made the biggest impression on Algeria, however. Today, Islam is the official state religion and is practiced by almost everyone in the country. *Islam* is an Arabic word that means "submission to God." It is related to other Arabic words, such as salām, which means "peace." Salām is often used as a greeting, instead of saying "hello."

God Is Called Allah

Muslims worship the same God as Christians and Jews. Muslims call God "Allah." God also has at least 99 other lyrical names in the Islamic tradition. Among the more poetic are Afûw (The Forgiver), Ahad (The One or The Only One), Âkhir (The End and Ultimate); Barr (The Source of Goodness); Hâdî (The Leader on the Right Path) and Wâsi' (The All-Embracing, The All-Pervading).

Algeria's Religions

Sunni Muslim	99%
Christian and Jewish	1%

There Is Only One God **93**

Followers of Islam are called Muslims. In Arabic, *Muslim* means a "servant" of God, as well as "one who surrenders" or "bows" to God.

Muslims believe that everything in nature is Islamic because all life follows the natural laws established by God. Therefore, a devout Muslim works hard to follow God's commands in everything he or she does throughout the day. There is no dividing line between daily life and religion or politics and religion. It is all wrapped together.

The Qur'an is the Muslim holy book. Muslims believe that the Qur'an is the actual word of God, as told to the Prophet Muhammad over a period of twenty-two years. By reading the Qur'an, young Algerians learn about many people and events that are also familiar to Jews and Christians through the Bible. While the details vary between the Qur'an and the Bible, both have stories about Adam, Noah, Abraham, Moses, Jesus, and John the Baptist.

White prayer beads on the Qur'an

The Prophet

Muhammad is the major prophet of Islam. He was born around A.D. 570 in Mecca, now a holy city in Saudi Arabia. As a young man, Muhammad disliked the pagan religions he encountered traveling around the Middle East. He spent much time praying and meditating. Muslims believe that in 610, the will of Allah was revealed to Muhammad by the angel Jibreel (Gabriel) outside Mecca. In the coming years, Muhammad is said to have received many more messages from God. These revelations were written down and became the Qur'an.

In 622, faced with persecution by nonbelievers, Muhammad fled to Medina, another city in Saudi Arabia, where he won converts to his cause. Muhammad skillfully combined negotiation and military muscle to become the strongest leader in the Arab world. Less than a century after his death in 632, Islam already had found its way from the Atlantic Ocean to China. Algeria was among the areas that fell under Arab Muslim control during this time.

In Islam, Arabic is the language used in prayer, whether the worshipper lives in Indonesia, India, the United States, or Canada. This is similar to when Jews pray in Hebrew or when traditional Roman Catholic masses are said in Latin.

There are two main branches of Islam, Sunni and Shia. Sunni Muslims make up about 99 percent of believers in Algeria. Some Berber groups practice a mystical form of Islam called Sufism, while others look to Muslim saints called marabouts for spiritual leadership.

The Grand Mosque in Mecca, Saudi Arabia

Besides the Qur'an, Islamic laws and customs are contained within sayings of the prophet called the Hadith and in the legal code of Shari'a. The rules found within the code forbid Muslims from gambling, drinking alcohol, and eating pork.

The Five Pillars of Islam

There are five basic beliefs, or "pillars," of Islam:

- There is no God but God (Allah in Arabic), and Muhammad is his prophet.
- Prayers must be said five times a day while facing Mecca.
- Generous help must be given to the poor.
- Fasting must occur during Ramadan, the ninth month of the Islamic year.
- Muslims must try to make a pilgrimage to Mecca at least once in their lives. This journey, called the hajj, takes place during Dhu Al-Hijjah, the twelfth month of the Muslim calendar.

Praying at the Mosque

The mosque is the Muslim "temple," the center of prayer. From its minaret, or tower, clergy call the faithful to prayer. Algiers has several major mosques, which long ago made the city a spiritual center of Muslim North Africa. Among the most famous is the sprawling Djemaa el Djedid mosque, which was built in 1660 by the Turks. Two blocks away is the Djemaa el Kebir, the Great Mosque, which dates to the eleventh century. It was built by Yusuf ibn Tashfin, a ruler during the Almoravid dynasty.

A minaret of a mosque in Reggane

Algeria's Religious Celebrations

Muslim religious holidays and festivals are timed according to local sightings of various phases of the moon, with dates changing each year.

The entire month of Ramadan is special. During Ramadan, Muslims fast from sunup to sundown. This follows the Qur'an preaching of self-restraint and reminds Muslims of the less fortunate who are constantly hungry and thirsty. Pregnant women, the ill, old people, and young children are not required to participate in the fast. Instead, they are to help feed the poor. At sundown during Ramadan, families sit down to a delicious meal. Laylat Al-Qadr, the Night of Power, is the most important night of Ramadan. It celebrates Muhammad receiving his first revelation. Aid al-Fitr, the Festival of the Breaking of the Fast, marks the end of the Ramadan fast. It involves prayer and visiting with friends and relatives.

Aid Al-Adha, the Holiday of the Sacrifice, is another major festival for Algerian Muslims. Each family sacrifices something, usually a sheep. Men say special prayers at the mosque, while the women prepare the sheep for dinner. A third of the meat is eaten at home, a third is given to the poor, and another third is given to a friend or to the neighborhood.

Another important holiday, Awwal Muharram, celebrates the Islamic New Year. Awwal Muharram commemorates Muhammad's trip away from Mecca, where he was being persecuted, to Medina, where he found acceptance and faithful followers.

The Ashura holiday commemorates the day Noah left the Ark after the Great Flood. It also marks the day the grandson of Muhammad, Husayn, was killed in a battle. Usually, the celebration involves fasting, helping the poor, and visiting family graves. Children love the celebration because they receive gifts and candy in memory of their deceased ancestors.

Al Mawlid Al-Nabi celebrates the birth of Muhammad. During this holiday in the Kabylie region of Algeria, an ox is killed and the meat shared among villagers. At night, children parade around the town with lighted candles mounted on reed stalks. They sing, "Today, the feast of the Prophet. The angels in heaven are pleased, and we are too." Afterward, at the evening meal, an extra spoon is placed on the table for any family member not at home. For instance, the father of the family might be working in France, or a son could be serving in the army on the Moroccan border.

Ibn Tashfin also founded the modern city of Tlemcen in northwest Algeria, though there had been earlier cities on the site. Tlemcen became one of Algeria's great Islamic cities, flourishing as a literary and governmental center from 1236 until 1553, when it fell under the control of the Ottoman Empire. Tlemcen is still beautiful, with tree-lined streets and productive vineyards. Many noted Algerian scholars and saints called the city their home. Today, the city skyline is dominated by the Great Mosque, which was built in 1136. Many of the region's early rulers were buried in a quiet corner of the square fronting the mosque. The Sidi Ben Hassan Mosque is much smaller and now houses the city's Museum of Antiquities. It is named after a famous fourteenth-century teacher.

Southeast of downtown Tlemcen is the mosque and gravesite of Sidi Bu Madyan (1126–1198), an early Islamic mystic and famous teacher who was born in Spain and moved to Algeria. In 1956, revolutionary leader Mohammed

Boukharouba took on the name Houari Boumedienne to honor Bu Madyan. Boumedienne was president of Algeria from 1965 to 1978.

Oran's most famous religious site is the Djemaa el Kebir mosque, down a hill from the city's main square, which was constructed in 1796. In 1900, the building was restored, and it is now a major religious attraction.

Other Religions

Jews and Christians are generally free to practice their faiths in Algeria as long as they pay their taxes, don't try to make converts, and don't interfere with Islam's religious practices. The government's Ministry of Religious Affairs requires other religions to obtain official recognition before they can conduct any services. Most non-Muslims are Methodists or belong to small sects of born-again evangelists. Other Protestant groups and the Roman Catholic Church are also active in Algeria. Most non-Muslims in Algeria live in the large cities.

The Basilica of Notre-Dame D'Afrique in Algiers

State Control of Religion

After gaining independence, the Algerian government took control of religious activities. The new constitution affirmed that Islam was the state religion and said that no laws that were against Islamic beliefs could be enacted. The state built new mosques and today, the Ministry of Religious Affairs is in charge of about five thousand mosques. Imams, the Islamic religious leaders, are trained and receive salaries from the government. Often the ministry even writes the imams' sermons. This ministry also makes sure that children have religious education in schools.

Some fervent Algerian Muslims want the state to enforce stricter rules that reflect traditional Muslim law. In 1991, Islamists nearly took over the government. The elections were set aside to prevent this from happening, setting off years of violent civil unrest that has killed one hundred fifty thousand people.

This rise in militant Islam has impacted Algerian society in other ways. Modesty in clothing, especially for women, is extremely important to the Islamists. Many Algerian women wear veils and long black dresses. Some do this to express their religious beliefs. Others feel that the clothing protects them from being harassed.

The Islamist movement has a wide national appeal. Islamists have attacked government corruption and presented ideas for tackling the lack of housing and jobs. Yet they also demand a crackdown on what they see as loose morality and a lack of serious attention paid to religious affairs. As such, Algeria is still attempting to find a safe middle ground for its citizens, based on conflicting beliefs on how to best serve God.

Life Is Art

ART PERMEATES ALL OF ALGERIAN LIFE. IN ALGERIA, art has been molded by tradition and culture, modified by a colonial experience, reshaped by a modern Arab mentality, and touched by religion. Many Algerians have found ways to bring all these complex details together and retain their individuality. Singer Houria Niati was born in 1948 near Algiers, but now lives in London. She expresses this cultural mix by writing songs in French, translating them into English, and then singing the lyrics in haunting Arabic. Niati is also a noted painter. At shows of her paintings, she often recites her own poetry to the accompaniment of synthesizers and a light show.

Rachid Koraichi has also incorporated his culture into art in an unusual way. In his calligraphy, he turns the Arabic alphabet into symbols of protest and revolution. Painter Zahir Abid moved to New York from his home in the Kabylie region of Algeria in the 1980s. One of his most whimsical paintings, *New York, Views from Africa*, shows giraffes looking almost like skyscrapers. Many of the animals wear pink and purple boots.

Opposite: **Men of the desert gather to play traditional music.**

A sculpture of the Roman emperor Augustus housed in the Archaeological Museum in Cherchel

Artists in Danger

Being an artist in Algeria has sometimes been dangerous, especially if he or she speaks out against religious or political oppression. The country's artists were especially targeted during the revolution against the French in the 1950s and the Islamist uprisings of the 1990s. One of Algeria's greatest writers, Tahar Djaout, was killed in 1993. After his murder, an unpublished novel called *The Last Summer of Reason* was found among his papers. It tells the story of a bookseller's struggle against militant Islam.

Kabyle singer Lounes Matoub

Singer Lounes Matoub was only forty-two years old when he was murdered by terrorists in 1998. Matoub was widely known for his pro-democracy positions and was among the strongest opponents of militant Islam. In one of his famous songs, translated as "Mute Algerian," he sang about oppression during the Boumedienne presidency. He wrote the song "The Gendarme of Shame" (*Gendarme* is French for "policeman") after being shot at by a policeman during a rally.

Other major Algerian entertainers who were gunned down because of their outspoken songs and political positions

Singer Cheb Hasni was killed in 1994.

include record producer and composer Rachid Baba-Ahmed and singers Cheb Hasni, Lila Amar, and Cheb Aziz. Aziz was only twenty-eight years old when he was killed. Poet Youcef Sebti and Abdelkader Alloula, manager of the National Theater, were also assassinated. Even students at the Algiers School of Fine Arts were targeted because their work was thought to be "decadent."

By the 2000s, terrorism in Algeria subsided somewhat, and the Algerian art scene again blossomed. The year 2003 was declared the "Year of Algeria" in France, with art and photography shows, musical productions, and theater. Algerian artists gained recognition elsewhere in the Western world. Abdallah Benanteur—a painter, engraver, and producer of art books decorated with watercolor and etchings—has received high praise.

Algeria's Literary World

Algeria has a long heritage of writers, dating back to ancient times. Lucius Apuleius (A.D. 125?–200?) was a Roman philosopher and writer, born in Madaurus in the kingdom of Numidia. He was most famous for writing *The Golden Ass*.

Many outsiders have written about Algeria. The French government sent novelist Alexander Dumas of *The Three Musketeers* fame to North Africa in 1846 to write about the French colony. His book, *Adventures in Algeria*, still provides a valuable glimpse into the country of that time. Isabelle Eberhardt, who was born in 1877 in Geneva, Switzerland, moved to North Africa, where

Below left: **Writer and philosopher Lucius Apuleius**

Below right: **Author Isabelle Eberhardt**

she became a Muslim and married an Algerian soldier. She traveled on horseback around Algeria, dressing as a man to pass safely through the country's most remote regions. Eberhardt died in a flash flood in 1904. Her diaries were eventually translated as *The Passionate Nomad*.

Algeria has produced an amazing array of writers, some working in French, others in Arabic, and still others in local dialects. Assia Djebar, a longtime history professor at the University of Algiers, is one of the best-known female writers of North Africa. Much of her work deals with women's issues. *Women of Algiers in Their Apartment* is a collection of stories about women who have survived colonialism only to find that their lives are more limited after the revolution. Djebar is also an award-winning filmmaker. Ahlam Mosteghanemi is the author of *Memory in the Flesh* (1985), the first Arabic-language novel published by an Algerian woman.

Mohammed Dib (1920–2003) was one of Algeria's most prolific writers and an important figure in world literature. His "Algerian trilogy" focuses on a large, poor family living in Algeria in the 1930s and 1940s. Dib was an innovative writer who tried a variety of techniques and explored different genres, including science fiction. Kateb Yacine is most famous for his 1956 novel *Nedjma*, which uses a fragmented story and multiple narrators to bring a mythic dimension to Algeria's struggle for independence.

Assia Djebar is one of North Africa's most famous writers.

Albert Camus

Throughout his life, Mouloud Mammeri (1917–1989) struggled for the recognition of the Amazigh Berber culture and language throughout North Africa. Today, the Amazigh have Web sites promoting their traditions. Several young Berbers living in the United States produce *The Amazigh Voice*, a quarterly publication with poems, stories, and essays from offices in Bloomington, Illinois.

Not all Algerian writers are of Arabic or Berber backgrounds. Albert Camus (1913–1960) was a French-Algerian novelist, essayist, and journalist. He was born in the French colonial city of Mondovi, now Drean, to a French father and a Spanish mother. He is perhaps most famous for his novel *The Stranger*. Camus won the 1957 Nobel Prize for Literature. The presenters noted that in his work, "clear-sighted earnestness illuminates the problems of the human conscience in our times."

Frantz Fanon (1925–1961) was a noted French psychiatrist and writer whose work influenced radical movements in the United States and Europe during the 1960s. In 1953, Fanon began working in a psychiatric ward in Algeria. He later became caught up in the Algerian revolution and was wounded in the fighting. He died of cancer in 1961, the same year that his most famous work, *The Wretched of the Earth*, was released. The book was based on his experiences during the Algerian war of independence.

Algerian Film

The film industry has a long heritage in North Africa, beginning with the first news shorts produced in 1909 in Egypt and the silent movies of the 1920s. During the revolution against France, many propaganda films were produced. It wasn't until the 1970s that the country's filmmakers moved beyond the story of the war to tackle other issues. Today, the Algerian film industry is small but strong. Merzak Allouache is one of the country's most famous filmmakers. His best-known movie, *Bab El Oued City*, tells the story of a poor Algiers neighborhood and the rise of brutal militant Islam. The film won the International Critics' Prize at the Cannes Film Festival in 1994. Mohammed Lakhdar Hamina is sometimes considered Algeria's greatest director. His film *Chronicle of the Years of Embers* received the Grand Prize at Cannes in 1976.

Music Old and New

Music has always had an important place in the Algerian social scene. In 1968, the National Institute of Music launched programs to support traditional music and dances and to ensure that folklore would be preserved. Poetry with musical accompaniment has long been popular. It is traditionally sung by men wearing *jellabas*, which are long white robes, and turbans known as *cheikhs*. The chanting singers also played *guellals*, drums made from a piece of piping with a skin at one end, and *gaspas*, flutes made of bamboo. In 1906, Mohammed Senoussi was the first to record this wild, vibrant street music.

Men in jellabas and cheikhs playing traditional music

Dancing to Rai

Rai (pronounced "rye"), Algeria's most popular music, originated in the 1930s as thousands of poor people made their way to the cities in search of work. From Algeria, rai spread across North Africa and to Europe. *Rai* literally means "a way of seeing," but it also can be interpreted as "a plan" or "a thought." As far back as the sixteenth century, Algerians would visit a wise man called a *shaykh* to seek his rai—his advice expressed as poetry. Today, that tradition comes down in song. Best of all, everyone loves dancing to the music.

Some of Algeria's best rai music now comes out of Oran, a major port with ferries going directly to Spain and France. Because of this, rai poetry has many influences, including French, Spanish, literary Arabic, rural Berber dialects, and street-tough city slang. Even elements of Jamaican reggae music have found their way into the rai sound.

Traditionally, instruments used for rai music were the *tbila*, a small drum beaten with a stick, and the *oud*, a twelve-string lutelike instrument. Later, accordions, banjos, and electric guitars were added. Mohammed Maghni brought in keyboards in the 1960s while part of an Algerian pop/rai group called the Students. Brothers Rachid and Fethi Baba introduced synthesizer and drum-machine sounds into rai in 1982.

A *cheb* (pronounced "shabb") is a male rai singer, while the women are called *chabas*. In Arabic, cheb translates to "young man," and *chaba* means "young woman." "The King of Rai," Cheb Khaled, was born in Oran and started recording at age fourteen. He made it big in the 1980s. But the Algerian government considered rai music subversive at the time, so Khaled emigrated to Paris. In 1992, his song "Didi" made him a superstar in France and with younger Algerians living around the world. In the 2000s, he began composing arrangements with hip-hop artists in the United States and Great Britain.

Safy Boutella is an Algerian rai musician and songwriter.

Young Algerians love music. In addition to traditional folk songs, they enjoy the hip-hop that has become popular throughout North Africa and in the Algerian communities in France. Much like older Algerian music, this new music deals with problems in the government and society. "I must speak the truth and give a voice to those who are mistreated . . . . We are like birds kept in a cage, thirsting for happiness and freedom," the group Intik sings. Kids flock to stores to buy CDs by Intik and other groups such as Brigade Anti-Massacre, Hamma Boys, and SOS. Many Algerian hip-hop groups use Algerian dialects in their songs, rather than rapping in French or English.

Sports

Soccer, or football, is the most popular sport in Algeria. Every major city in the country has a soccer stadium, but kids also play ball in empty fields, back lots, and school grounds.

Algeria began participating in the Olympics in 1964. Eighty Algerians qualified for the 2004 Games in Athens, Greece. They included fencers, boxers, weight lifters, wrestlers, swimmers, tennis players, and other athletes. In past Olympics, Algeria's runners have been particularly successful. Noureddine Morceli won the gold medal in 1996 in the 1,500-meter event. Morceli was so good that he was never defeated in the 1,500-meter event in the forty-five races he ran between 1992 and 1996. At one point, Morceli held the world records for all distances from 1,500 meters to 3,000 meters. A star athlete who appeared at the

2000 Olympic Games was Nouria Merah-Benida. She won gold in the women's 1,500-meter race there, something her fellow Algerian Hassiba Boulmerka had achieved at the 1992 Olympics.

Other respected Algerian athletes include boxer Hocine Soltani, who won a gold medal at the 1996 Olympics and a bronze at the 1992 Games. Then there's in-line skating champion Taig Khris, who was born in Algeria and grew up in Paris. One of the world's top extreme sports competitors, Khris specializes in freestyle ramp board skating. Khris, who now lives in the United States, speaks five languages, plays the piano, and is an excellent tennis player.

Algeria swept the field with 227 medals at the tenth annual Pan-Arab Games, held in 2004 in Algiers. The star of the show was Baya Rahouli, who captured four gold medals. Rahouli won the women's 100-meter hurdles and the 100-

Runner Nouria Merah-Benida

meter flat, as well as the triple jump and long jump titles. Fans went wild as she racked up win after win.

Some popular sports in Algeria are not Olympic events. In the desert, camel races are sometimes held. Riders gallop along a field that can be 2 miles (3 km) or more in length. It takes several minutes for the animals to get up to speed, but once they get going, they can reach speeds of up to 40 miles (65 km) per hour. In another Algerian sport, riders on horses gallop as fast as they can while shooting at a target.

A growing number of tourists are taking advantage of Algeria's Atlas Mountains for skiing. One of the most popular areas is Chréa, 44 miles (70 km) south of Algiers. The area also has excellent walking trails for summertime exercise. Most Algerians take their vacations in August, flocking to the coastal areas near Algiers and Oran to swim, water ski, and sail on the Mediterranean Sea. There is always something to see and enjoy in Algeria.

A Day of
Celebration

ALI ZEROUAL COULD HARDLY CONTROL HIS EXCITEMENT as he ate his breakfast of *chakchouka*, a flavorful dish of poached eggs mixed with peppers. The wonderful perfume of cooked garlic, onions, and paprika filled the tiny kitchen in the predawn morning. To help Ourida, his mother, Ali had diced the red and green peppers that made the base of the meal. Ourida then assembled a bed of the cooking peppers in a pan and placed the eggs on top of the mixture. After she covered the skillet, the eggs had time to cook through. Those ten minutes seemed the longest that Ali had ever experienced. He was really hungry. But the dish was soon ready, and he used big slices of his mother's thick, crusty bread to mop up all the delicious leftovers.

Opposite: **A young girl dancing near Touggourt**

Women preparing a meal for the family

After prayers and breakfast, Ali would not eat again until that evening. It was the middle of Ramadan, and Ali and his friends were now old enough to fast for the month. Although Ali realized the importance of self-restraint by not eating from dawn to dusk, he was always glad when his mother eventually signaled that supper was ready. "No good Muslim will touch food so long as he is able to distinguish a black from a white thread," she always warned. He hoped that his mother would make her wonderful fish soup for the night meal. But that was hours away. He had just finished breakfast, and the whole day was open for play.

Soup's On

Algerian fish soup is a typical Mediterranean dish. Every country that borders the Mediterranean has some variation on it. In Algeria, fish soup is a staple at home and is often served in restaurants and small cafés. It is especially popular along the waterfronts of Algiers, Oran, Béjaia, Tizi-Ouzou, and smaller coastal villages. Fish soup is inexpensive to prepare and makes a hearty meal when served with chunks of freshly made bread, a dish of olives, and platter of cheese. Every family has a favorite recipe. While there are many variations that use different herbs, this is a common version.

Ingredients:

1 tablespoon olive oil
1 large Spanish onion, chopped
3 cloves garlic, minced
2 peeled whole tomatoes
1 teaspoon paprika
Sprigs of parsley and thyme

2 large potatoes
3 stalks celery, diced
A pinch of crushed saffron
Salt and pepper, to taste
2 pounds firm white fish
8 cups chicken broth, or 4½ cups fish stock

Heat the oil in a pan and add the onion and garlic. Cook until the onions are soft. Add the spice and remaining vegetables. Cut the fish into one-inch pieces. Lay the pieces on top of the vegetable mixture and add just enough broth or stock to cover the fish. Bring to a low simmer and cook over very low heat for one hour, or until the fish flakes. Skim off any residue from the surface of the soup and serve.

The Martyr's Monument honors Algeria's struggle for independence.

Today, November 1, was special. It was the fiftieth anniversary of the start of Algeria's successful revolt against French rule in 1954. It was a national holiday, so schools were closed and many workers did not have to report to their jobs. From the kitchen window, Ali could already hear motorists honking their car horns, even though it was still early. Everyone was ready to celebrate.

President Abdelaziz Bouteflika addresses Algeria's top officials.

There would be fireworks that evening at the Martyr's Monument. This would honor all the patriots who fought for Algeria's freedom—such as Grandpa Hussein, who lived in the city of Ghardaia, south of Algiers. Ali's grandfather now worked as a restaurant manager in the Hotel Napht off the Rue Ahmed Talbi. Ali liked to visit Ghardaia, especially because his grandpa's kitchen staff knew him. They usually gave him extra helpings of his favorite dish—chicken and couscous, tiny steamed pasta. Every holiday, Ali's family would telephone grandpa to see how he enjoyed the day. The older man always had plenty of stories to tell Ali about his days fighting for the revolution.

From the radio in the background, Ali heard a new song. The famous singer Warda al-Jazairia had written the tune in honor of the revolution. The announcer then reminded listeners that Algerian president Abdelaziz Bouteflika was awarding the singer with a National Order of Merit during a big celebration later that day at the Mohamed Boudiaf sports complex. He told how her father's hotel in Paris was a favorite hideaway for many young Algerian nationalists in the 1940s. There they would discuss plans for the revolution. The radio then played the president's anniversary message encouraging neighborliness and peace. To mark the day, the president even pardoned a number of political prisoners. In a gesture of peace, he canceled the military parade traditionally held on this anniversary.

Ali's father, Ahmed Zeroual, had already left the house well before his son finished breakfast. After his morning prayers at the Ketchaoua mosque, Zeroual planned to meet Ali's two uncles at a coffeehouse to play a round of dominos and talk about world events. In the afternoon, they were to visit the Hamman Sidna, a public bath built in the sixteenth century. There the three men would relax with a steam bath and a massage. It was an opportunity they did not want to miss. Usually, they were very busy during the day. All three were lucky to have good jobs at the city's Port Said. Ali's father operated a huge crane, unloading and loading cargo from

Men in a Tlemcen café

An Algerian family preparing to enjoy tea

the freighter ships that stopped in Algiers. Uncle Ahmed was an accountant in the office of a transport company and talked to businesspeople all over the world every day. Uncle Houari managed the ticket office at the ferry landing off the Boulevard Zighout Youssef. It was always fun for Ali to visit the bustling harbor and to dream of working on a ship when he grew up.

Ourida was cleaning up the house, sweeping out its six rooms and straightening the rugs and pillows in preparation for Ali's aunts, who were planning a visit for mint tea and conversation. Preparing the tea on a holiday was always a ceremony in itself. Ourida brought out her special silver teapots from the cabinet. Hot water, tea, and several spoonfuls of sugar were mixed as Ali's mother poured the brew from pot to pot until it was frothy. She then served the tea in delicate glasses that were only used on special occasions. Although Ali loved his aunts, this would be no place for a twelve-year-old boy. He was glad he was going to play soccer with his friends. After cleaning the table of his breakfast dishes, he needed to hurry. He was almost late for the game they planned for that morning.

Caring for Kids in Algeria

Some children in Algeria have had their lives torn apart by war, terrorism, or natural disasters. Many Algerian volunteers, governmental programs, and international organizations contribute to the efforts to care for these children.

The United Nations Volunteers program celebrated International Volunteer Day on December 6, 2003, by honoring Foundation Mahfoud Boucebci, an organization that assists children who are victims of violence. Boucebci was a psychologist who was killed in Algeria's civil strife of the 1990s.

After World War II, Austrian Hermann Gmeiner saw the need for a safe place where young people could put their lives back together. In 1949, he started an organization called SOS Kinderdorf International and began building villages around the world where children who had lost their families could feel safe.

After a devastating earthquake in 1980, Gmeiner's organization decided to build a village in Algeria. Initially, the village was in Algiers. In the 1990s, construction of a new community began in Draria, 8 miles (13 km) south of Algiers. The little "town," which began operating in 1992, now has ten family houses and an SOS-Kindergarten, plus a meeting hall and workshop. There is also a house for the staff. About ninety children live at Draria at any given time. They are admitted to the village after careful screening. Natural brothers and sisters are not separated. Children are accepted from infancy until the age of ten.

Every child has an SOS mom who lives with them. The children grow up together as if they were brothers and sisters. This home setting gives each child a feeling of love and stability.

Women in traditional clothing shop for food and other essentials.

As Ali ran out of his house, he spotted a platter of *samsa* that had been baked for supper. He loved the almond-honey flavor of the triangular pastry. With that vision on his mind, the Ramadan fasting would be particularly hard today. Luckily, his attention was quickly diverted as he watched the crowd of men and boys waving Algerian flags and singing the national anthem as they paraded along the street in front of his house. He saw only a few women shoppers. They were dressed in flowing robes and headscarves.

Ali raced down the street with his soccer ball tucked tightly under his arm. Dodging the traffic on Rue Docteur, Ali soon saw his pals on the corner near the park where they planned to play. When everyone was finally together, the boys immediately started talking about Algerian soccer coach Ali Fergani and his selection of a twenty-four-man national team, the Desert Foxes. The team was going to play a friendly

Children playing soccer

match against Senegal later in the month. Already, the team had a 1-1 draw with Rwanda in an important 2006 World Cup qualifying match. All the guys were excited, hoping that Fergani could bring some life to Algeria's football fortunes. Since Ali was usually a goalkeeper, he loved comparing the skills of Mohamed Benhamou, Karim Soula, and Merouane Abdouni, the goalies for the Desert Foxes. One of Ali's friends had the latest copy of *Le Buteur*, Algiers' football newspaper, which discussed the team's prospects.

Finally, Ali and his friends started their game. During the rousing match, Ali admirably defended his goal, which consisted of two jackets set apart the regulation width of 24 feet (7.3 m). Around noon, the players paused for prayers. Each boy knelt on the ground facing east, the direction of the holy city of Mecca. All around them, men were doing the same.

After the game, Ali said goodbye to his buddies and headed toward home. He had promised to do some grocery shopping for his mom before it was time for supper. As he did his errands at the shops in the neighborhood near his house, he caught snatches of the anniversary celebration being broadcast on televisions and radios. Many people were talking about the fireworks planned for that evening at the Martyr's Monument. Ali wished he could go see the display, but he had a language arts test at school the next morning and his parents didn't want him out late. They all planned to watch the festivities at home on television, however.

Martyr's Monument

Visiting Martyr's Monument

Ali's class at school had already been to the Martyr's Monument several times. They always rode bus Number 32 from the Place Audin to near the memorial. They would get off the bus and

When it isn't Ramadan, Algerian street vendors offer a variety of delicious foods in Victory Park.

walk to the monument, a large structure with three upward sweeping arcs. Because of his service to his country between 1955 and 1962, Grandpa Hussein had taken part in the monument's dedication in 1982, which marked the twentieth anniversary of Algerian independence. Ali was always proud when he visited the monument, which honored what his grandfather had done as a young man. After picnicking on the grass beneath the monument, Ali and his school friends usually visited the Musée National du Jihad and looked at the displays covering the struggle for freedom.

Victory Park stretched beyond the Martyr's Monument. In the middle of the park were several restaurants where the kids

could get a soft drink and sit in the outside patio. It was too expensive, however, to eat in El-Boustane or the Dar Hizia. Nobody ever seemed to have enough dinars in their pockets, and the waiters would eventually shoo them away.

If it hadn't been Ramadan, street vendors selling kebabs would be all around. They offered delicious skewered lamb and vegetables cooked over open grills. The kebabs were sometimes not as good as the food at Fast Burger, in Bois des Arcades at Riadet-Fet'h, but if Ali was hungry, he still might have two. Sometimes, actors rehearsed at the Théatre du Verdure, a nearby open-air theater, and the kids could watch as they ate. Field trips from school were always fun.

Gathered Around the Television

That evening, after prayers, homework, supper, and an extra piece of samsa, Ali and his parents gathered around the phone for a long chat with Grandpa Hussein. They then turned on their small television set to watch the ceremonies at the Martyr's Monument. Everyone laughed whenever Ali's mom oohed and aahed as the fireworks display exploded in the clear night sky above the monument. Near the harbor, a cannon salute was echoed by the sound of ships' sirens offshore. Ali was very tired, but he was still too wound up to sleep. As midnight came, more ships blasted their horns as Ali and his family and neighbors went outside to cheer. From over the rooftops, the final blasts of red, white, and yellow fireworks signaled that everything was all right in Ali's world.

There would be plenty to talk about at school tomorrow.

Timeline

Algerian History

Prehistoric people make rock art on cliff walls at Tassili N'Ajjer.	ca. 5500 B.C.
Phoenicians build outposts in what is now Algeria.	1100s B.C.
Carthage asserts its influence in Algeria.	800s B.C.
Massinisa, the leader of the Berber kingdom of Numidia, dies.	148 B.C.
Rome takes control of Numidia.	105 B.C.
Vandals gain control of North Africa.	A.D. 430
Byzantine rule begins in North Africa.	533
Arabs sweep into Algeria.	600s
The Rustamid Dynasty, the first Muslim state in Algeria, is founded.	777
Spain establishes forts along the Algerian coast.	1505–1511
Khayr al-Din (Barbarossa) helps the Ottoman Turks establish themselves in Algeria.	1514–1529

World History

2500 B.C.	Egyptians build the Pyramids and the Sphinx in Giza.
563 B.C.	The Buddha is born in India.
A.D. 313	The Roman emperor Constantine recognizes Christianity.
610	The Prophet Muhammad begins preaching a new religion called Islam.
1054	The Eastern (Orthodox) and Western (Roman) Churches break apart.
1066	William the Conqueror defeats the English in the Battle of Hastings.
1095	Pope Urban II proclaims the First Crusade.
1215	King John seals the Magna Carta.
1300s	The Renaissance begins in Italy.
1347	The Black Death sweeps through Europe.
1453	Ottoman Turks capture Constantinople, conquering the Byzantine Empire.
1492	Columbus arrives in North America.
1500s	The Reformation leads to the birth of Protestantism.

Algerian History

France invades Algeria.	**1830**
Algeria becomes part of France.	**1848**
Allied troops invade Algeria.	**1942**
The Algerian revolution begins.	**1954**
Oil is discovered at Hassi Messaoud.	**1956**
Algeria gains independence from France.	**1962**
Algeria joins OPEC.	**1969**
An earthquake in El Asnam (now called Ech-Cheliff) kills 5,000 people.	**1980**
Riots result in economic reforms and a new constitution.	**1988**
Unrest in Algeria results in 150,000 deaths.	**1990s**
Drought ravages Algerian agriculture.	**2000**
An earthquake kills more than 2,000 people.	**2003**

World History

1776	The Declaration of Independence is signed.
1789	The French Revolution begins.
1865	The American Civil War ends.
1914	World War I breaks out.
1917	The Bolshevik Revolution brings communism to Russia.
1929	Worldwide economic depression begins.
1939	World War II begins, following the German invasion of Poland.
1945	World War II ends.
1957	The Vietnam War starts.
1969	Humans land on the moon.
1975	The Vietnam War ends.
1979	Soviet Union invades Afghanistan.
1983	Drought and famine in Africa.
1989	The Berlin Wall is torn down, as communism crumbles in Eastern Europe.
1991	Soviet Union breaks into separate states.
1992	Bill Clinton is elected U.S. president.
2000	George W. Bush is elected U.S. president.
2001	Terrorists attack World Trade Towers, New York, and the Pentagon, Washington, D.C.
2003	The U.S. invades Iraq.

Fast Facts

Official name: People's Democratic Republic of Algeria

Capital: Algiers

Official language: Arabic

Algiers

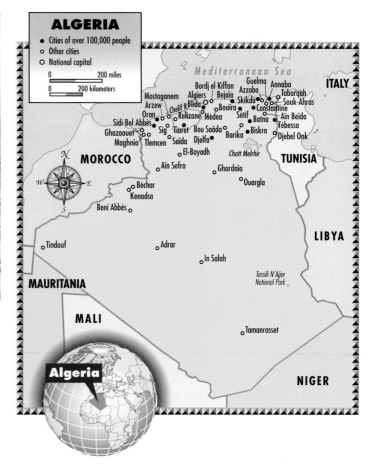

Algeria's flag

Official religion:	Islam
Government:	Republic
Head of state:	President
Area:	919,595 square miles (2,381,741 sq km)
Borders:	The Mediterranean Sea to the north; Libya and Tunisia to the east; Mauritania, Morocco, and Western Sahara to the west; Niger and Mali to the south.
Length of coastline:	750 miles (1,200 km)
Lowest elevation:	Chott Melrhir, 102 feet (31 m) below sea level
Highest elevation:	Mount Tahat, 9,573 feet (2,918 m)
National population (2005 est.):	32,531,853

Population of largest cities:

Algiers	1,886,000
Oran	1,110,000
Constantine	808,000

Ethnic population:

Arab-Berber	83%
Berber	16%
European	1%

The Sahara Desert

Martyr's Monument

Famous landmarks: ▶ *Grotte Karstique de Ghar Boumâaza*, Tlemcen

▶ *Djemaa el Kabir Mosque*, Oran

▶ *Martyr's Monument*, Algiers

▶ *Port Said Harbor*, Algiers

▶ *Tassili N'Ajjer National Park*, Djanet

▶ *Palace of Ahmed Bey*, Constantine

Industry: Oil and gas are the mainstays of the economy, accounting for roughly 60 percent of budget revenues, 30 percent of gross domestic product, and more than 95 percent of export earnings. Algeria has the world's fifth-largest reserves of natural gas and is the second-largest gas exporter. Iron, lead, zinc, copper, calamine, antimony, phosphate, mercury, and lignite coal are also mined. Algeria manufactures steel, cement, and electrical components. It also exports olives, wine, and citrus crops.

Currency: The basic unit of money is the dinar. In August 2005, 73 dinars equaled one U.S. dollar.

Weights and measures: Metric system

Literacy rate: 70 percent

Dinar

Algerian men

Albert Camus

Famous People:

Augustine *Church father*	(354–430)
Ahmed Ben Bella *Algeria's first president*	(1919–)
Hassiba Boulmerka *Track athlete*	(1968–)
Sidi Bu Madyan *Islamic mystic, Algeria's patron saint*	(1126–1198)
Albert Camus *Nobel Prize–winning novelist*	(1913–1960)
Mohammed Dib *Novelist*	(1920–2003)
Khayr al-Din (Barbarossa) *Sea captain who helped Ottoman Turks become established in Algeria*	(ca. 1483–1546)
Assia Djebar *Writer and film director*	(1936–)
Noureddine Morceli *Runner*	(1970–)
Abd al-Qadir *Algerian revolutionary leader*	(1807–1883)

To Find Out More

Books

▶ Gordon, Matthew. *Islam*. New York: Facts on File, 2001.

▶ Hoy-Goldsmith, Diane. *Celebrating Ramadan*. New York: Holiday House, 2001.

▶ Kagda, Falaq. *Algeria*. Tucson, Ariz.: Benchmark Books, 1997.

▶ Mahaney, Ian F. *Taig Khris: In-Line Skating Champion*. New York: PowerKids Press, 2005.

Web Sites

▶ **U.S. Department of State, Bureau of Consular Affairs**
www.travel.state.gov/travel
For information on travel in Algeria.

▶ **CIA World Fact Book**
www.cia.gov/cia/publications/factbook/geos/ag
For geographic, financial, government, and social information on Algeria.

▶ **Africanet.Com**
www.africanet.com/countries/algeria
To learn more about Algeria's history, geography, language, customs, and climate.

Embassies

▶ **Embassy of the People's Democratic Republic of Algeria**
2118 Kalorama Road, NW
Washington, DC 20008
202/265-2800

Index

Page numbers in *italics* indicate illustrations.

Meet the Author

ARTIN HINTZ has written nearly one hundred books for young readers and adults, including many volumes in the Enchantment of the World series. He has also written books about subjects ranging from monster trucks to training elephants.

Hintz is also a journalist. He publishes *The Irish American Post*, an online news magazine that focuses on the Irish and Irish Americans. He manages the Mountjoy Writers Group, an international news syndicate. He belongs to several professional journalism associations and is the past president and chairman of the board of the Society of American Travel Writers. He is active in the Society of Professional Journalists and is a member of the Committee to Protect Journalists, an organization that tracks journalists in trouble with their local governments.

To research *Algeria*, Hintz conducted interviews, visited the library to find books and articles, and uncovered extensive information on the Internet.

Hintz and his wife, Pam, live on a small farm in Wisconsin, where they raise chickens and the occasional pig. Tom, a Maine coon cat, is a new addition to their household.

Photo Credits